MORE Bible PUZZLES

SEEK AND FIND

AGES 8 & UP

For information regarding the CPSIA on this printed material call:
203-595-3636 and provide reference # LANC-315751

Rainbow Publishers • P.O. Box 261129 • San Diego, CA 92196
www.RainbowPublishers.com

MORE Bible Puzzles

SEEK AND FIND

AGES 8 & UP

John Hudson Tiner

This book is dedicated to Jayetta, Zachary and Oliver.

MORE BIBLE PUZZLES: SEEK AND FIND
©2011 by Rainbow Publishers, seventh printing
ISBN 10: 1-58411-050-3
ISBN 13: 978-1-58411-050-7
Rainbow reorder# RB38431
RELIGION / Christian Ministry / Children

Rainbow Publishers
P.O. Box 261129
San Diego, CA 92196
www.RainbowPublishers.com

Certified Chain of Custody
SUSTAINABLE FORESTRY INITIATIVE
Promoting Sustainable Forest Management
www.sfiprogram.org

Scriptures are from the *Holy Bible: New International Version* (North American Edition), ©1973, 1978, 1984 by the International Bible Society. Used by permission of Zondervan Bible Publishers.

Printed in the United States of America

Contents

Introduction.....................................7

God Made Everything.....................9

Trouble in a Beautiful Garden 11

Noah Builds an Ark.........................13

A Promise to Abraham 15

A Test for Abraham.........................17

Two Brothers.................................19

Joseph's New Coat.........................21

Baby Moses 23

Food from Heaven.........................25

Ten Laws from God.........................27

The Walls of Jericho.......................29

Gideon's Army.............................31

Boaz and Ruth 33

God Speaks to Little Samuel 35

David and the Giant 37

A Beautiful Temple.........................39

Elijah and the Widow's Son...............41

Naaman Is Made Well......................43

David's Beautiful Song.....................45

The Fiery Furnace 47

The Lions' Den.............................49

Jonah in the Fish 51

The Angel Visits Mary 53

The Shepherds Hear About Jesus...........55

Wise Men Worship Jesus 57

Jesus as a Boy in the Temple..............59

Jesus Is Baptized 61

The Apostles 63

Jesus Raises a Boy from the Dead 65

Food for 5,000..............................67

Walking on Water..........................69

Paying the Tax..............................71

The Good Shepherd........................73

The Good Samaritan 75

Jesus Visits Mary and Martha 77

A Son Leaves Home 79

Jesus Blesses Little Children 81

A Blind Man Receives Sight 83

Zacchaeus Climbs a Tree 85

A Hero's Welcome..........................87

Eating in an Upper Room 89

Peter Denies Jesus..........................91

The Terrible Deed 93

Jesus Lives!................................95

introduction

*M*ore Bible Puzzles: Seek and Find is a collection of word search puzzles based on favorite stories from throughout the Bible, both Old and New Testaments. The puzzles – with their triple challenges – are an enjoyable way to learn more about important events in the Bible. The secret phrases were chosen to show that the Old and New Testaments complement one another. These word searches make a good teaching resource. They provide an incentive for members of a class to study God's Word. They are great for individual enjoyment, too.

THREE CHALLENGES

1. Find the hidden words. Key words from well-known Bible stories are hidden in each puzzle. A hidden word may be spelled in any direction: up, down, left, right or diagonally. Some hidden words may cross one another and share words. As you find a word, draw a line through it in the puzzle grid and mark it from the word list.

2. Discover the secret phrase. The secret phrase is spelled out with the letters left over after you have found the hidden words. Write the unused letters in the blanks to discover the secret phrase.

3. Recall the Bible story. Use the hidden words and secret phrase to help you bring out the important ideas in the Bible story. Reading down each column and then across will give the words in the order in which they appear in the Bible story. Scripture references are provided for all puzzles and for the secret phrases. (You may want to read the passages in your Bible to recall the stories in detail.)

The New International Version (NIV) of the Bible is used for these puzzles.

Enjoy!

God Made Everything
Genesis 1

From the first book in the Old Testament (Genesis) to the last book in the New Testament (Revelation), we learn that God made everything. After you find the words in the puzzle grid, write the unused letters in the blanks to spell out what Revelation says about God and His creation.

▬ ▬

BEGINNING	MORNING	THIRD	LIVING	INCREASE
CREATED	FIRST	SEASONS	BIRDS	SUBDUE
HEAVENS	EXPANSE	GREATER	FIFTH	SIXTH
EARTH	SEPARATED	LESSER	IMAGE	
LIGHT	SECOND	STARS	BLESSED	
EVENING	PLANTS	FOURTH	FRUITFUL	

▬ ▬

```
L I V I N G F O G R F
M O R N I N G N Y I E
B D O U S I I C R G R
I R N R S N O S A E R
R E A O N E T M I E S
D T S I C V I N E U L
S A G N A E C T F D E
E E D A E R S T O B S
B R P P E V I C U U E
L G L A L U A R R S R
T H S I R A E E T F S
I E G F N A N A H I I
G H D R I H T T R F X
T E S N A P X E S T T
S B L E S S E D D H H
```

Secret Phrase

... _____ _____ _____

_____ _____ . . . .   **– Revelation 4:11**

9

God Made Everything

Answers

Secret Phrase

. . . For you created all things. . . .

~ Revelation 4:11

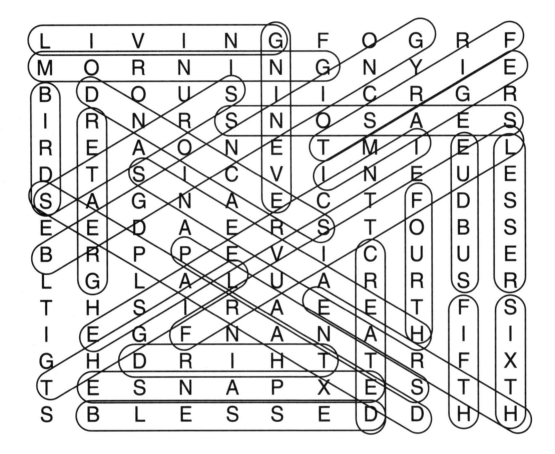

Example: Find BEGINNING by counting down 9 rows and then beginning in the first column.

BEGINNING (9,1)   CREATED (9,8)   HEAVENS (12,9)   EARTH (11,7)   LIGHT (10,5)

EVENING (7,6)   MORNING (2,1)   FIRST (1,11)   EXPANSE (14,8)   SEPARATED (7,1)

SECOND (8,7)   PLANTS (9,4)   THIRD (13,7)   SEASONS (4,11)   GREATER (10,2)

LESSER (5,11)   STARS (7,1)   FOURTH (7,9)   LIVING (1,1)   BIRDS (3,1)   FIFTH (11,10)

IMAGE (6,7)   BLESSED (15,2)   FRUITFUL (12,4)   INCREASE (5,9)   SUBDUE (10,10)

SIXTH (11,11)

Trouble in a Beautiful Garden
Genesis 3:1-24

Although evil entered the world when Adam and Eve sinned, the Bible says that a stronger one than Satan would destroy evil. Jesus is stronger than Satan! After you find the words, the unused letters spell out a New Testament verse that describes what would happen to Satan.

▬ ▬ ▬ ▬ ▬ ▬ ▬ ▬ ▬ ▬ ▬ ▬ ▬ ▬ ▬ ▬ ▬ ▬ ▬ ▬

SERPENT	PLEASING	BELLY	GROUND
CRAFTY	HUSBAND	ENMITY	THORNS
EYES	WALKING	WOMAN	THISTLES
OPENED	GARDEN	HEAD	SWEAT
GOOD	COOL	HEEL	FLAMING
EVIL	AFRAID	COMMANDED	SWORD

▬ ▬ ▬ ▬ ▬ ▬ ▬ ▬ ▬ ▬ ▬ ▬ ▬ ▬ ▬ ▬ ▬ ▬ ▬ ▬

```
G  D  O  D  O  F  P  E  A  C  S  E
D  E  N  E  P  O  W  I  L  W  L  T
G  D  N  U  O  R  G  S  E  O  H  O
N  N  D  H  N  F  L  A  M  I  N  G
I  A  I  U  E  C  T  R  S  U  S  H
K  M  A  S  S  E  Y  T  F  A  R  C
L  M  R  B  A  N  L  W  S  E  T  O
A  O  F  A  E  E  R  A  O  N  T  O
W  C  A  N  S  L  L  O  E  M  D  L
G  A  R  D  E  N  L  P  H  I  A  A
N  U  O  Y  N  I  R  Y  D  T  E  N
E  O  E  R  V  E  Y  O  U  Y  H  R
G  S  F  E  S  W  O  R  D  E  E  T
```

Secret Phrase

(The) __ __ __   __ __   __ __ __ __ __   __ __ __ __ __

__ __ __ __   __ __ __ __ __   __ __ __ __ __

__ __ __ __ __ __   __ __ __ __ __   __ __ __ __ . - Romans 16:20

11

Trouble in a Beautiful Garden

Answers

Secret Phrase

(The) God of peace will soon crush Satan under your feet.

~ Romans 16:20

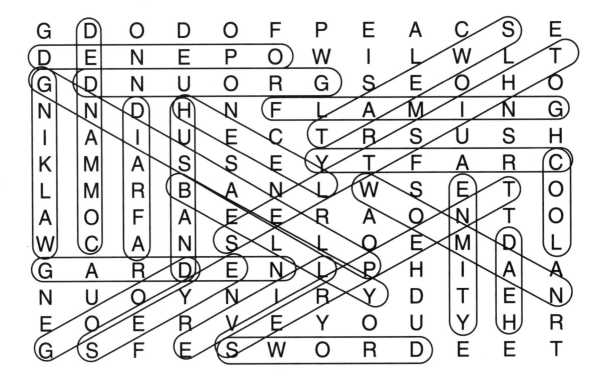

Example: Find SERPENT by counting down 13 rows and then across 5 columns.

SERPENT (13,5) CRAFTY (6,12) EYES (10,5) OPENED (2,6) GOOD (13,1) EVIL (13,4)

PLEASING (10,8) HUSBAND (4,4) WALKING (9,1) GARDEN (10,1) COOL (6,12)

AFRAID (9,3) BELLY (7,4) ENMITY (7,10) WOMAN (7,8) HEAD (12,11) HEEL (4,4)

COMMANDED (9,2) GROUND (3,7) THORNS (11,10) THISTLES (2,12) SWEAT (1,11)

FLAMING (4,6) SWORD (13,5)

Noah Builds an Ark
Genesis 6:9-22; 7:1-12

By following God's command, Noah built an ark – a type of boat – that kept him, his wife, their three sons and their wives safe during the flood. After you find the words in the puzzle grid, use the remaining letters to discover what the New Testament book of Hebrews says about Noah.

ACCOUNT	CYPRESS	CREATURE	FLOODGATES
NOAH	WOOD	SONS	HEAVENS
RIGHTEOUS	PITCH	WIFE	OPENED
FILLED	FLOODWATERS	WIVES	FORTY
VIOLENCE	BIRD	SPRINGS	DAYS
DESTROY	ANIMAL	DEEP	NIGHTS

```
H  B  Y  F  A  I  S  E  V  I  W
A  S  P  R  I  N  G  S  T  H  I
O  P  E  N  E  D  S  V  N  O  F
N  H  E  T  A  Y  I  N  S  L  E
R  C  D  H  A  O  I  N  O  A  T
I  T  R  D  L  G  E  O  F  N  D
G  I  B  E  H  V  D  O  U  I  E
H  P  N  T  A  W  R  O  W  M  L
T  C  S  E  A  T  C  S  O  A  L
E  U  H  T  Y  C  U  I  O  L  I
O  L  E  T  A  B  I  R  D  N  F
U  R  A  Y  O  R  T  S  E  D  S
S  S  E  R  P  Y  C  N  A  R  K
```

Secret Phrase

___ ___ __ ___ ___ ___ ___ ___ ___ ___ ··· ___ ___ ___ ___ ___

___ ___ ___ ___ ___.   **- Hebrews 11:7**

13

Noah Builds an Ark

Answers

Secret Phrase

By faith Noah. . .built an ark.

~ Hebrews 11:7

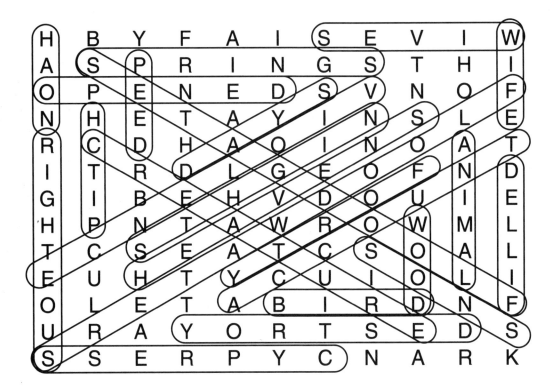

Example: Find ACCOUNT by counting down 11 rows and then across 5 columns.

ACCOUNT (11,5) NOAH (4,1) RIGHTEOUS (5,1) FILLED (11,11) VIOLENCE (3,8)

DESTROY (12,10) CYPRESS (13,7) WOOD (8,9) PITCH (8,2) FLOODWATERS (3,11)

BIRD (11,6) ANIMAL (5,10) CREATURE (5,2) SONS (9,8) WIFE (1,11) WIVES (1,11)

SPRINGS (2,2) DEEP (5,3) FLOODGATES (11,11) HEAVENS (10,3) OPENED (3,1)

FORTY (6,9) DAYS (6,4) NIGHTS (4,8)

A Promise to Abraham
Genesis 15:1-6, 26:4-5

God told Abraham that through his children all of the nations of the earth would be blessed. The blessing was fulfilled by Jesus when He came into the world to take away the sins of those who live for Him. After you find the words, discover what the New Testament book of James says about Abraham.

WORD	SHIELD	CHILDREN	BELIEVED	NATIONS
LORD	REWARD	HEIR	CREDITED	EARTH
CAME	SOVEREIGN	HEAVENS	RIGHTEOUSNESS	BLESSED
ABRAM	REMAIN	COUNT	DESCENDANTS	OBEYED
VISION	CHILDLESS	STARS	NUMEROUS	COMMANDS
AFRAID	INHERIT	OFFSPRING	LANDS	LAWS

```
A  B  R  A  H  A  M  B  G  E  S  L  S  I
S  U  O  R  E  M  U  N  E  S  N  S  O  V
T  H  C  R  E  D  I  T  E  D  E  E  V  D
A  D  I  A  F  R  A  I  D  N  V  G  E  O
R  D  E  E  P  S  A  R  S  A  A  N  R  D
S  H  D  S  L  E  D  U  I  L  E  C  E  W
A  S  F  E  C  D  O  N  C  E  H  N  I  A
V  F  M  O  V  E  H  E  A  I  H  A  G  L
O  I  U  A  T  E  N  R  L  M  L  T  N  D
E  N  S  H  R  D  I  D  D  G  M  I  R  E
T  O  G  I  R  B  L  L  A  D  R  O  L  Y
D  I  T  A  O  E  A  I  E  N  W  N  C  E
R  S  W  F  S  N  R  H  I  B  T  S  A  B
D  E  S  S  E  L  B  C  L  A  W  S  M  O
R  E  M  A  I  N  E  N  H  T  R  A  E  D
```

Secret Phrase

···__ __ __ __ __ __ __   __ __ __ __ __ __ __ __   __ __ __···

__ __ __ __   __ __   __ __ __   __ __ __ __ __ __ __   __ __ __ ,__

__ __ __ __ __ __ __ __ .   **– James 2:23**

15

A Promise to Abraham

Answers

Secret Phrase

. . . Abraham believed God . . . and he was called God's friend.

~ James 2:23

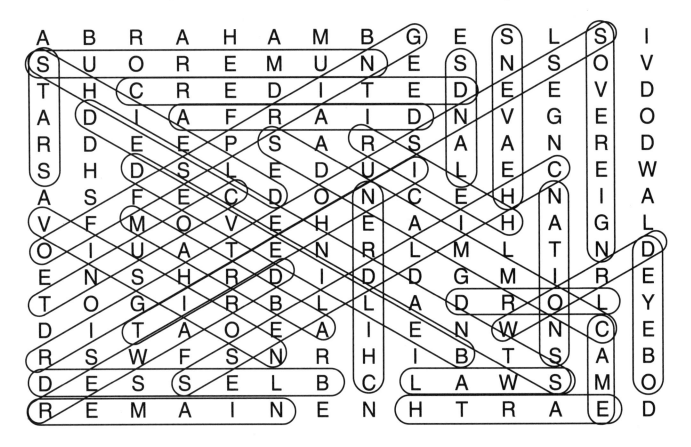

Example: Find WORD by counting down 12 rows and then across 11 columns.

WORD (12,11) LORD (11,13) CAME (12,13) ABRAM (12,7) VISION (8,1) AFRAID (4,4)

SHIELD (2,1) REWARD (15,1) SOVEREIGN (1,13) REMAIN (15,1) CHILDLESS (6,12)

INHERIT (6,9) CHILDREN (14,8) HEIR (8,11) HEAVENS (7,11) COUNT (7,5) STARS (2,1)

OFFSPRING (9,1) BELIEVED (13,10) CREDITED (3,3) RIGHTEOUSNESS (13,1)

DESCENDANTS (4,2) NUMEROUS (2,8) LANDS (6,10) NATIONS (7,12) EARTH (15,13)

BLESSED (14,7) OBEYED (14,14) COMMANDS (12,13) LAWS (14,9)

A Test for Abraham
Genesis 22:1-19

Abraham believed God's promises. He did what God told him to do, and he was rewarded because of his faith. God tested Abraham's faith by telling him to sacrifice his son Isaac. Abraham trusted God to make even this difficult task turn out well – and it did! The secret phrase reveals more of what the New Testament book of James tells about Abraham.

ABRAHAM	ISAAC	ANGEL	DESCENDANTS	OBEYED
MOUNTAINS	ALTAR	LOOKED	NUMEROUS	
LAMB	WOOD	THICKET	SAND	
PROVIDE	REACHED	HORNS	SEASHORE	
BUILT	HAND	BURNT	NATIONS	
BOUND	KNIFE	OFFERING	BLESSED	

```
B  U  R  N  T  A  D  N  U  O  B  B
B  M  A  L  R  S  A  M  T  B  L  A
H  A  I  E  G  T  D  A  H  E  E  M
B  U  M  R  I  N  E  H  I  Y  G  L
B  I  S  O  A  A  I  A  C  E  N  N
L  E  N  H  U  D  V  R  K  D  A  U
E  S  R  S  D  N  C  B  E  L  E  M
S  A  O  A  O  E  T  A  T  F  K  E
S  N  H  E  O  C  K  A  N  F  R
E  D  D  S  W  S  R  O  I  S  G  O
D  E  H  C  A  E  R  F  O  N  I  U
P  R  O  V  I  D  E  O  D  L  S  S
```

Secret Phrase

… __ __ __ __ __ __ __   __ __ __ __ __ __ __   __ __ __ . . . .

– James 2:23

A Test for Abraham

Answers

Secret Phrase

. . . Abraham believed God. . . .

~ James 2:23

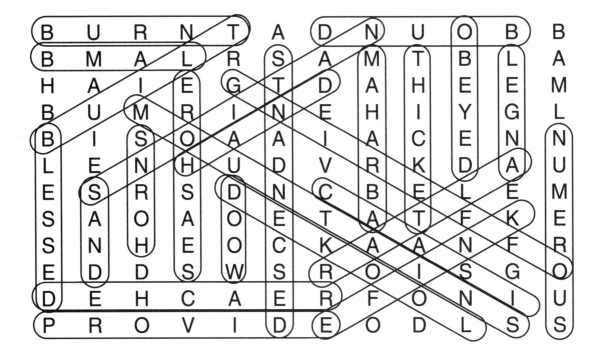

Example: Find ABRAHAM by counting down 8 rows and then across 8 columns.

ABRAHAM (8,8) MOUNTAINS (4,3) LAMB (2,4) PROVIDE (12,1) BUILT (5,1)

BOUND (1,11) ISAAC (11,11) ALTAR (6,11) WOOD (10,5) REACHED (11,7) HAND (6,4)

KNIFE (8,11) ANGEL (6,11) LOOKED (12,10) THICKET (2,9) HORNS (9,3) BURNT (1,1)

OFFERING (10,12) DESCENDANTS (12,6) NUMEROUS (5,12) SAND (7,2)

SEASHORE (10,4) NATIONS (1,8) BLESSED (5,1) OBEYED (1,10)

Two Brothers
Genesis 25:21-34

In Old Testament times, the oldest brother was given the largest share of his father's possessions after his father died. Twin brothers Jacob and Esau were the sons of Isaac and Rebekah. Although Esau was the older, he did not end up with his inheritance. The secret phrase tells what happened to it.

▬▬ ▬ ▬▬ ▬ ▬ ▬ ▬ ▬ ▬ ▬ ▬ ▬ ▬ ▬ ▬ ▬ ▬ ▬ ▬▬ ▬

ISAAC	TWIN	JACOB	TENTS	BIRTHRIGHT
REBEKAH	HAIRY	SKILLFUL	COOKING	
NATIONS	GARMENT	OPEN	STEW	
OLDER	ESAU	COUNTRY	FAMISHED	
SERVE	BROTHER	PLAIN	SELL	
YOUNGER	HEEL	STAYING	DESPISED	

▬▬ ▬ ▬▬ ▬ ▬ ▬ ▬ ▬ ▬ ▬ ▬ ▬ ▬ ▬ ▬ ▬ ▬ ▬ ▬▬ ▬

```
N  R  E  B  E  K  A  H  E  S  B
E  I  Y  I  A  O  L  D  E  R  U
P  D  W  R  E  G  N  U  O  Y  S
O  E  E  T  I  E  E  T  P  R  O
L  S  D  H  V  A  H  S  L  T  G
H  P  K  R  S  E  H  S  A  N  I
G  I  E  I  R  I  N  S  I  U  I
N  S  N  G  L  O  M  K  N  O  T
I  E  H  H  I  L  O  A  I  C  E
Y  D  E  T  H  O  F  S  F  R  N
A  I  A  E  C  T  A  U  T  A  T
T  N  E  M  R  A  G  L  L  E  S
S  L  J  A  C  O  B  N  C  E  W
```

Secret Phrase

··· __ __ __ __ ··· __ __ __ __   __ __ __

__ __ __ __ __ __ __ __ __ __ __ __ __ __ ____ ···· — Hebrews 12:16

Two Brothers

Answers

Secret Phrase

. . . Esau . . . sold his inheritance. . . .

~ Hebrews 12:16

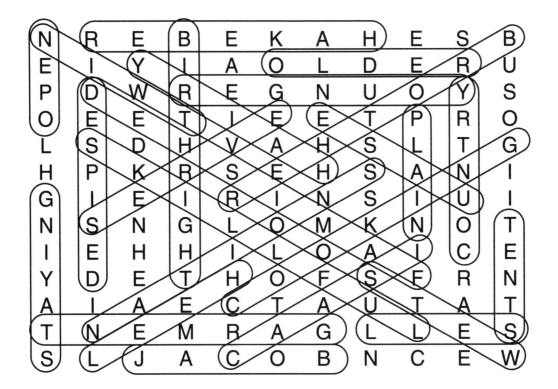

Example: Find ISAAC by counting down 9 rows and then across 9 columns.

ISAAC (9,9) REBEKAH (1,2) NATIONS (12,2) OLDER (2,6) SERVE (8,2)

YOUNGER (3,10) TWIN (4,4) HAIRY (6,7) GARMENT (12,7) ESAU (4,7)

BROTHER (1,11) HEEL (10,5) JACOB (13,3) SKILLFUL (5,2) OPEN (4,1)

COUNTRY (9,10) PLAIN (4,9) STAYING (13,1) TENTS (8,11) COOKING (11,5)

STEW (10,8) FAMISHED (10,9) SELL (12,11) DESPISED (3,2) BIRTHRIGHT (1,4)

Joseph's New Coat
Genesis 37:1-11

Jacob was Isaac's son and Abraham's grandson. Jacob had 12 sons, but his favorite was Joseph. Use the words in this puzzle to help you tell the story of what happened when Jacob gave Joseph a new coat. The secret phrase reveals what Joseph's brothers did to him out of jealousy.

▬ ▬

JACOB	TENDING	ORNAMENTED	SHEAVES	ELEVEN
STAYED	FLOCKS	ROBE	STOOD	STARS
CANAAN	LOVED	BROTHERS	UPRIGHT	FATHER
JOSEPH	MORE	HATED	BOWED	REBUKED
YOUNG	MADE	DREAM	REIGN	JEALOUS
SEVENTEEN	RICHLY	BINDING	RULE	

▬ ▬

```
Y  T  H  E  B  F  P  S  T  A  R  S  A
T  L  M  R  I  A  R  E  B  U  K  E  D
Y  D  H  A  N  T  I  V  B  O  W  E  D
G  O  E  C  D  H  A  A  S  O  Y  L  R
C  N  U  T  I  E  H  E  T  A  R  U  E
B  M  I  N  N  R  V  H  T  E  B  R  S
E  R  A  D  G  E  G  S  I  S  O  S  O
L  L  O  E  N  I  M  G  H  M  C  K  D
E  J  O  T  R  E  N  A  A  N  A  C  L
V  S  E  P  H  D  T  E  N  P  J  O  H
E  E  U  H  P  E  S  O  J  R  V  L  I
N  N  T  O  D  E  R  G  Y  E  O  F  P
T  J  E  A  L  O  U  S  D  O  O  T  S
```

Secret Phrase

___ ___ ___   ___ ___ ___ ___ ___ ___ ___...___ ___ ___...

___ ___ ___ ___ ___   ___ ___ ___   ___ ___ ___ ___ ___....

A Pleasing Sacrifice

Answers

Secret Phrase

The patriarchs . . . sold . . . (Joseph) . . . into Egypt. . . .

~ Acts 7:9

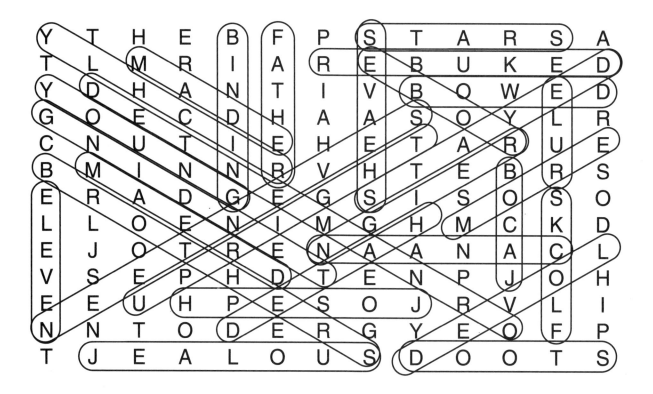

Example: Find JACOB by counting down 10 rows and then across 11 columns.

JACOB (10,11) STAYED (7,8) CANAAN (9,12) JOSEPH (11,9) YOUNG (3,1)

SEVENTEEN (4,9) TENDING (10,7) FLOCKS (12,12) LOVED (9,13) MORE (8,10)

MADE (2,3) RICHLY (6,6) ORNAMENTED (12,11) ROBE (5,11) BROTHERS (6,1)

HATED (8,9) DREAM (10,6) BINDING (1,5) SHEAVES (7,8) STOOD (13,13)

UPRIGHT (11,3) BOWED (3,9) REIGN (5,11) RULE (6,12) ELEVEN (7,1)

STARS (1,8) FATHER (1,6) REBUKED (2,7) JEALOUS (13,2)

Baby Moses
Exodus 2:1-10

One of the favorite Bible stories in the Old Testament is about Moses when he was a baby. His mother did some special things to keep Moses safe from Pharaoh. See if you can tell the story using the words below as a guide. After you find the words in the puzzle grid, write the unused letters in the blanks to spell out the secret phrase.

▬ ▬ ▬ ▬ ▬ ▬ ▬ ▬ ▬ ▬ ▬ ▬ ▬ ▬ ▬ ▬ ▬ ▬ ▬ ▬

LEVITE	COATED	PHARAOH	BABY	MOSES
WOMAN	PITCH	DAUGHTER	CRYING	WATER
FINE	PLACED	BATHE	SORRY	
CHILD	REEDS	ATTENDANTS	HEBREW	
PAPYRUS	NILE	SLAVE	NURSE	
BASKET	SISTER	OPENED	MOTHER	

▬ ▬ ▬ ▬ ▬ ▬ ▬ ▬ ▬ ▬ ▬ ▬ ▬ ▬ ▬ ▬ ▬ ▬ ▬ ▬

```
A   M   O   C   E   S   R   U   N   S
E   T   W   E   R   B   E   H   A   S
P   P   T   A   A   Y   R   S   M   E
H   A   R   E   T   S   I   S   O   N
A   O   P   E   N   E   D   N   O   M
R   T   B   Y   E   D   R   D   G   S
A   W   A   A   R   D   A   E   R   T
O   E   B   N   T   U   S   N   O   E
H   T   Y   D   G   H   S   F   T   K
M   O   T   H   E   R   E   I   H   S
D   E   T   A   O   C   V   N   C   A
A   E   N   I   L   E   A   E   T   B
R   C   H   I   L   D   L   L   I   F
R   A   Y   R   R   O   S   I   P   D
```

Secret Phrase

···__ __ __ __ __ __ __ , __ __ __ __ __ __ __ __ __ __··· __ __ __

__ __ __ __   __ __ __ __ __ __ __ __ __ ....   — Hebrews 11:23

23

Baby Moses

Answers

Secret Phrase

. . . Moses' parents . . . were not afraid. . . .

~ Hebrews 11:23

```
A  M  O  C  E  S  R  U  N  S
E  T  W  E  R  B  E  H  A  S
P  P  T  A  A  Y  R  S  M  E
H  A  R  E  T  S  I  S  O  N
A  O  P  E  N  E  D  N  W  M
R  T  B  Y  E  D  R  D  G  S
A  W  A  A  R  D  A  E  R  T
O  E  B  N  T  U  S  N  O  E
H  T  Y  D  G  H  S  F  T  K
M  O  T  H  E  R  E  I  H  S
D  E  T  A  O  C  V  N  C  A
A  E  N  I  L  E  A  E  T  B
R  C  H  I  L  D  L  L  I  F
R  A  Y  R  R  O  S  I  P  D
```

Example: Find LEVITE by counting down 13 rows and then across 5 columns.

LEVITE (13,5) WOMAN (5,9) FINE (9,8) CHILD (13,2) PAPYRUS (3,1) BASKET (12,10)

COATED (11,6) PITCH (14,9) PLACED (14,9) REEDS (4,3) NILE (12,3) SISTER (4,8)

PHARAOH (3,1) DAUGHTER (6,8) BATHE (6,3) ATTENDANTS (1,1) SLAVE (14,7)

OPENED (5,2) BABY (6,3) CRYING (1,4) SORRY (14,7) HEBREW (2,8) NURSE (1,9)

MOTHER (10,1) MOSES (5,10) WATER (2,3)

Food from Heaven

Exodus 6:1-11

God gave Moses the task of leading the Israelites from slavery in Egypt to the Promised Land. However, the people had to cross a desert. Although they were free from the harsh life in Egypt, they complained that they were without food in the desert. Some even wanted to turn back to Egypt. But God gave them food in a special way. Circle the words, then write the unused letters on the blanks to find out whom this special food represented.

ISRAELITE	AARON	DEATH	TWICE	APPEARED
COMMUNITY	EGYPT	BREAD	MUCH	CLOUD
DESERT	MEAT	HEAVEN	EVENING	
GRUMBLED	FOOD	GATHER	MORNING	
AGAINST	BROUGHT	SIXTH	GLORY	
MOSES	STARVE	PREPARE	LORD	

```
T  H  C  G  N  I  N  E  V  E  G  E
B  H  M  O  R  N  I  N  G  R  A  R
N  E  T  A  M  E  E  V  R  A  T  S
E  D  O  X  G  M  Y  L  P  P  H  F
V  G  O  Y  I  R  U  P  O  E  E  D
A  I  P  D  O  S  E  N  T  R  R  S
E  T  I  L  E  A  R  S  I  P  D  A
H  H  G  S  R  L  N  B  B  T  A  C
E  W  O  E  D  I  B  D  R  R  Y  L
H  M  D  O  A  E  T  M  O  E  C  O
O  M  E  G  C  S  A  N  U  O  A  U
D  O  A  I  W  N  E  T  G  R  F  D
F  R  W  H  C  U  M  O  H  M  G  H
E  T  A  D  E  S  E  R  T  V  E  N
```

Secret Phrase

___ ____ __ ___ __ ___

___ ____ ____ ____

_____.   **- John 6:33**

Food from Heaven

Answers

Secret Phrase

The bread of God is he who comes down from heaven.

~ John 6:33

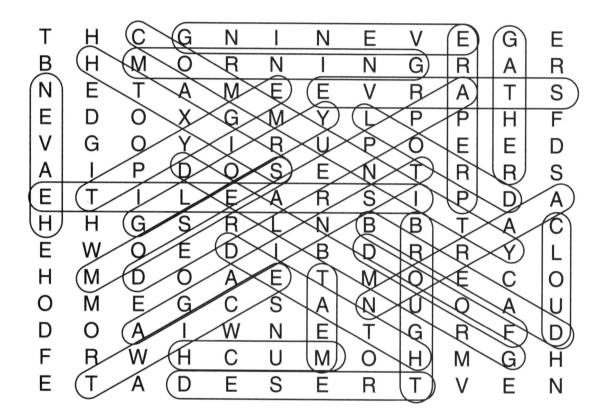

Example: Find ISRAELITE by counting down 7 rows and then across 9 columns.

ISRAELITE (7,9) COMMUNITY (1,3) DESERT (14,4) GRUMBLED (13,11) AGAINST (12,3)

MOSES (10,2) AARON (7,12) EGYPT (3,6) MEAT (13,7) FOOD (12,11) BROUGHT (8,9)

STARVE (3,12) DEATH (9,5) BREAD (8,8) HEAVEN (8,1) GATHER (1,11) SIXTH (6,6)

PREPARE (7,10) TWICE (14,2) MUCH (13,7) EVENING (1,10) MORNING (2,3)

GLORY (8,3) LORD (4,8) APPEARED (3,10) CLOUD (8,12)

Ten Laws from God

Exodus 20:1-17

The 10 laws from God are known as the "Ten Commandments." They are a perfect guide to how we should live for God and with others. Can you say the Ten Commandments? The words below are clues to the 10. Write the unused letters in the blanks to discover a new commandment from Jesus.

LORD	NAME	RESTED	ADULTERY	NEIGHBOR
GODS	REMEMBER	HONOR	STEAL	COVET
IDOL	SABBATH	FATHER	GIVE	
WORSHIP	HOLY	MOTHER	FALSE	
JEALOUS	LABOR	MURDER	TESTIMONY	
MISUSE	SEVENTH	COMMIT	AGAINST	

```
R  A  N  E  W  C  O  W  M  M  A  E
R  E  S  T  E  D  O  H  N  D  V  I
E  O  H  G  I  R  L  T  V  I  E  S
H  Y  B  T  S  N  I  A  G  A  U  T
T  O  U  H  O  L  R  B  B  O  G  E
A  A  I  C  G  M  E  B  L  O  O  A
F  P  D  V  O  I  M  A  D  E  R  L
O  N  N  U  D  M  E  S  U  S  I  M
C  F  A  R  L  J  M  N  E  A  Y  U
O  A  O  M  N  T  B  I  D  O  L  R
V  L  O  S  E  V  E  N  T  H  O  D
E  S  H  O  N  O  R  R  T  H  H  E
T  E  S  T  I  M  O  N  Y  E  R  R
```

Secret Phrase

__ ___ _____ _ ____

___: _____ ___ _____.

- John 13:34

Ten Laws from God

Answers

Secret Phrase

A new command I give you: Love one another.

~ John 13:34

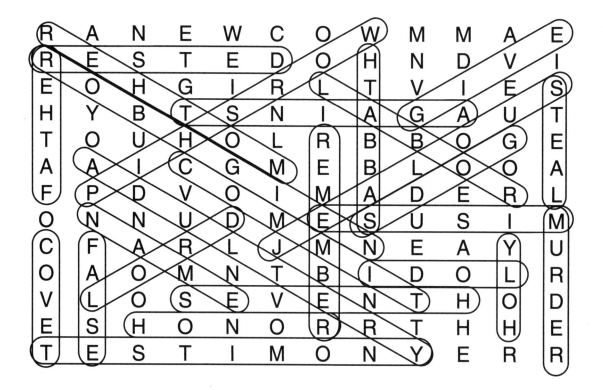

Example: Find LORD by counting down 11 rows and then across 2 columns.

LORD (11,2) GODS (5,11) IDOL (10,8) WORSHIP (1,8) JEALOUS (9,6) MISUSE (8,12)

NAME (8,2) REMEMBER (5,7) SABBATH (8,8) HOLY (12,11) LABOR (3,7)

SEVENTH (11,4) RESTED (2,1) HONOR (12,3) FATHER (7,1) MOTHER (6,6)

MURDER (8,12) COMMIT (6,4) ADULTERY (6,2) STEAL (3,12) GIVE (4,9)

FALSE (9,2) TESTIMONY (13,1) AGAINST (4,10) NEIGHBOR (9,8) COVET (9,1)

The Walls of Jericho
Joshua 6:8-21

When the Israelites crossed into the Promised Land, they came to Jericho, a city with strong walls all around it. Rather than attacking the city, God told His people to march around the city, shout and blow trumpets. Find out what happened by placing the unused letters on the secret phrase lines.

JOSHUA	MORNING	AROUND	SPARED	DESTROYED
PEOPLE	ONCE	SEVEN	SOUNDED	
PRIESTS	RETURNED	TIMES	SHOUTED	
BLOWING	CAMP	DAYBREAK	WALL	
TRUMPETS	EARLY	CIRCLED	COLLAPSED	
MARCHED	CARRYING	RAHAB	CITY	

```
S  O  U  N  D  E  D  D  B  S  C  Y
Y  T  I  C  F  S  E  M  I  T  A  A
S  D  E  H  C  R  A  M  I  S  R  T
D  E  S  P  A  L  L  O  C  E  R  H
T  E  V  P  M  R  H  K  T  I  Y  E
S  J  S  E  P  U  A  U  L  R  I  G
H  O  W  T  N  E  R  H  L  P  N  N
O  S  A  L  R  N  L  T  A  I  G  I
U  H  L  B  E  O  E  P  W  B  S  N
T  U  Y  D  E  A  Y  O  O  O  F  R
E  A  C  I  R  C  L  E  D  E  J  O
D  E  R  L  I  B  N  C  D  H  P  M
O  F  Y  E  L  A  R  O  U  N  D  L
```

Secret Phrase

___ ___   ___ ___ ___ ___   ___ ___ ___   ___ ___ ___ ___   ___ ___

___ ___ ___ ___ ___ ___ ___   ___ ___ ___.   – Hebrews 11:30

29

The Walls of Jericho

Answers

Secret Phrase

By faith the walls of Jericho fell.

~ Hebrews 11:30

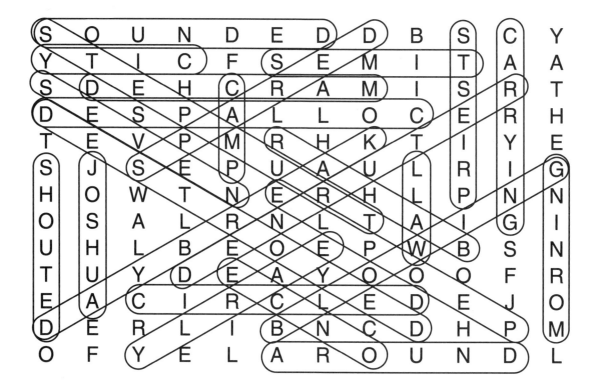

Example: Find JOSHUA by counting down 6 rows and then across 2 columns.

JOSHUA (6,2) PEOPLE (12,11) PRIESTS (7,10) BLOWING (12,6) TRUMPETS (8,8)

MARCHED (3,8) MORNING (12,12) ONCE (13,8) RETURNED (3,11) CAMP (3,5)

EARLY (9,7) CARRYING (1,11) AROUND (13,6) SEVEN (3,1) TIMES (2,10)

DAYBREAK (12,1) CIRCLED (11,3) RAHAB (5,6) SPARED (6,3) SOUNDED (1,1)

SHOUTED (6,1) WALL (9,9) COLLAPSED (4,9) CITY (2,4) DESTROYED (4,1)

Gideon's Army
Judges 7:1-22

Gideon was a hero of faith. He had a large and powerful army, but God told him to go into battle with only 300 men. Despite the army's small size, Gideon won the battle! He and his men could not boast about their own strength. Instead, they knew that the victory belonged to God. Find the secret phrase to see how Gideon and other Old Testament heroes were remembered in the New Testament book of Hebrews.

GIDEON	FEAR	DRINK	HUNDRED	LORD
MANY	REMAINED	LAPPED	NIGHT	CAMP
BOAST	WATER	MOUTHS	TRUMPETS	CRYING
STRENGTH	SEPARATE	GIVE	TORCHES	FLED
SAVED	TONGUES	MIDIANITES	SHOUTED	
TREMBLES	KNEEL	THREE	SWORD	

```
W   H   O   B   E   F   L   E   D   C   A
D   S   E   U   G   N   O   T   R   M   E
P   R   T   S   E   H   C   R   O   T   O
W   N   I   R   E   V   I   G   L   F   T
E   O   D   N   E   L   W   A   T   E   R
L   E   E   N   K   N   B   R   F   A   U
U   D   R   O   W   S   G   M   E   R   M
M   I   D   I   A   N   I   T   E   S   P
G   G   N   L   L   I   A   M   H   R   E
N   D   U   A   N   R   A   O   A   N   T
I   E   H   P   A   I   U   U   B   N   S
Y   V   M   P   N   T   G   T   A   T   Y
R   A   E   E   E   T   T   H   R   E   E
C   S   D   D   B   O   A   S   T   L   E
```

Secret Phrase

... ___ ___   ___ ___ ___ ___   ___ ___ ___ ___

___ ___   ___ ___ ___ ___ ___ ___ ___ .   – Hebrews 11:34

31

Gideon's Army

Answers

Secret Phrase

. . .who became powerful in battle.

~ Hebrews 11:34

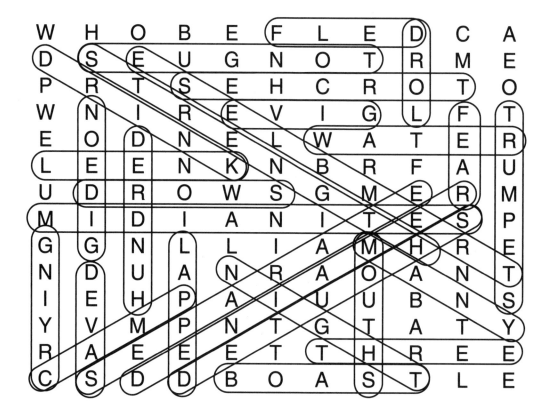

Example: Find GIDEON by counting down 9 rows and then across 2 columns.

GIDEON (9,2) MANY (9,8) BOAST (14,5) STRENGTH (2,2) SAVED (14,2)

TREMBLES (10,11) FEAR (4,10) REMAINED (7,10) WATER (5,7) SEPARATE (14,2)

TONGUES (2,8) KNEEL (6,5) DRINK (2,1) LAPPED (9,4) MOUTHS (9,8) GIVE (4,8)

MIDIANITES (8,1) THREE (13,7) HUNDRED (11,3) NIGHT (10,5) TRUMPETS (4,11)

TORCHES (3,10) SHOUTED (8,10) SWORD (7,6) LORD (4,9) CAMP (14,1)

CRYING (14,1) FLED (1,6)

Boaz and Ruth
Ruth 2:1-12

Why does the Bible devote an entire book to the story of Ruth? She was a woman from the country of Moab who traveled to the land of Israel. Although a poor foreigner, she married a wealthy man who lived in Bethlehem. Ruth was the great-grandmother of King David, one of whose descendants was Mary, Jesus' mother. Find the secret phrase to see how Ruth began her family.

RUTH	YOUNG	STAY	FAVOR	UNDER
LEFTOVER	WOMAN	THIRSTY	FOREIGNER	WHOSE
GRAIN	MOAB	DRINK	REPAY	WINGS
FIELDS	NAOMI	BOWED	RICHLY	REFUGE
HARVESTERS	GATHER	GROUND	REWARDED	
BOAZ	SHEAVES	FOUND	LORD	

```
B  W  O  A  I  Z  T  O  Y  A  T  S
O  O  H  M  F  K  D  L  T  R  R  D
U  M  O  O  T  H  E  R  H  E  E  L
G  A  U  A  S  F  W  N  I  D  A  E
N  N  F  B  T  E  O  I  R  N  N  I
D  N  U  O  R  G  B  A  S  U  K  F
L  S  V  O  R  D  W  R  T  S  T  H
O  E  E  O  Y  E  E  G  Y  S  E  H
R  C  V  V  R  R  I  C  H  L  Y  W
D  A  A  Z  A  O  B  G  M  E  A  I
F  E  G  U  F  E  R  H  N  I  P  N
S  W  I  G  A  T  H  E  R  E  E  G
F  E  H  A  R  V  E  S  T  E  R  S
```

Secret Phrase

____ _____ _____ ____ ____

_____ ____ _____.

- Ruth 4:13

Boaz and Ruth

Answers

Secret Phrase

Boaz took Ruth and she became his wife.

~ Ruth 4:13

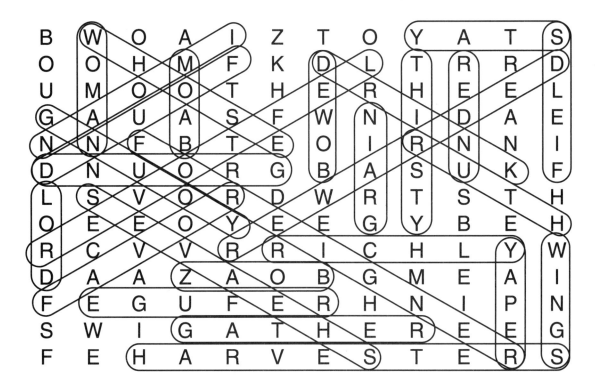

Example: Find RUTH by counting down 5 rows and then across 9 columns.

RUTH (5,9) LEFTOVER (2,8) GRAIN (8,8) FIELDS (6,12) HARVESTERS (13,3)

BOAZ (10,7) YOUNG (8,5) WOMAN (1,2) MOAB (2,4) NAOMI (5,1) GATHER (12,4)

SHEAVES (13,8) STAY (1,12) THIRSTY (2,9) DRINK (2,7) BOWED (6,7) GROUND (6,6)

FOUND (2,5) FAVOR (11,1) FOREIGNER (5,3) REPAY (13,11) RICHLY (9,6)

REWARDED (9,5) LORD (7,1) UNDER (6,10) WHOSE (1,2) WINGS (9,12) REFUGE (11,7)

God Speaks to Little Samuel
1 Samuel 3

The boy Samuel was training to be a priest. One night he heard a voice. He ran to the other room thinking that Eli, his teacher, had called. "Here I am," Samuel said. But Eli explained that Samuel had heard the voice of the Lord. Eli said the next time, Samuel should reply, "Speak, Lord, for your servant is listening." Samuel listened to God. Find the secret phrase to see what happened to Samuel because of his faith.

SAMUEL	REVEALED	LISTENING	FAILED	PROPHET
ANSWERED	THIRD	EARS	RESTRAIN	
CALLED	TIME	TINGLE	DOORS	
AGAIN	REALIZED	JUDGE	AFRAID	
DOWN	SPEAK	FAMILY	VISION	
WORD	SERVANT	CONTEMPTIBLE	GREW	

```
R  D  E  L  L  A  C  A  S  A  D  C
E  I  G  D  I  M  N  S  R  O  O  D
V  A  D  U  E  S  Y  E  W  N  V  R
E  R  U  N  W  L  T  N  T  D  I  I
A  F  J  E  I  N  I  E  L  E  S  H
L  A  R  M  A  A  M  A  N  Z  I  T
E  E  A  V  C  P  R  O  F  I  O  N
D  F  R  T  T  I  N  T  U  L  N  A
S  E  T  I  N  G  L  E  S  A  E  G
S  P  B  I  P  R  O  P  H  E  T  A
D  L  E  U  M  A  S  T  D  R  R  I
E  O  G  A  R  E  G  R  E  W  O  N
W  I  N  F  K  A  O  V  A  O  R  W
I  T  H  T  H  W  E  L  O  E  R  D
```

Secret Phrase

... __ __ __ __ __ __   __ __ __ __ __ __ __ __ __   __ __

__ __ __ __ __ __ ... __ __   __ __ __ __ __   __ __ __ __   __ __ __

__ __ __ __ __ ....   – 1 Samuel 2:26

God Speaks to Little Samuel

Answers

Secret Phrase

. . . Samuel continued to grow…in favor with the Lord. . . .

~ 1 Samuel 2:26

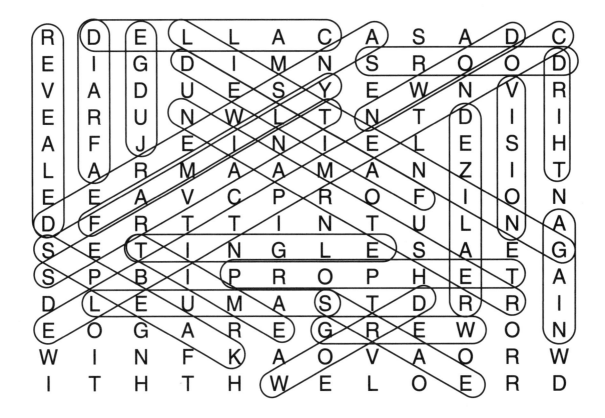

Example: Find SAMUEL by counting down 11 rows and then across 7 columns.

SAMUEL (11,7) ANSWERED (1,8) CALLED (1,7) AGAIN (8,12) DOWN (1,11)

WORD (14,6) REVEALED (1,1) THIRD (6,12) TIME (9,3) REALIZED (11,10)

SPEAK (9,1) SERVANT (10,1) LISTENING (1,4) EARS (14,10) TINGLE (9,3)

JUDGE (5,3) FAMILY (8,2) CONTEMPTIBLE (1,12) FAILED (7,9) RESTRAIN (11,11)

DOORS (2,12) AFRAID (6,2) VISION (3,11) GREW (12,7) PROPHET (10,5)

David and the Giant
1 Samuel 17

A champion is a person who defends a group of people against an enemy. David was a champion. As a young man, he accepted the challenge to go up against Goliath, a feared Philistine giant. David did not wear armor, and his only weapon was a slingshot. Yet David succeeded because God guided the smooth stone from his slingshot to its target. The secret phrase tells what David said to Saul about this challenge.

PHILISTINES	TALL	SAUL	LION	STONES
FORCES	STOOD	TERRIFIED	BEAR	FOREHEAD
GOLIATH	SHOUTED	DAVID	RESCUED	KILLED
OVER	SUBJECTS	YOUNGEST	LORD	
NINE	SERVE	SHEEP	DELIVER	
FEET	DEFY	FEAR	SMOOTH	

```
D  E  T  U  O  H  S  O  F  Y  P  O
E  I  D  E  L  I  V  E  R  H  U  D
F  R  V  L  R  E  A  G  I  T  S  R
Y  E  A  A  R  R  O  L  R  O  K  O
Y  T  V  A  D  L  I  D  N  O  I  L
O  D  N  S  I  S  E  F  T  M  L  W
U  A  N  A  T  U  H  I  I  S  L  L
N  E  T  I  C  C  L  E  E  E  E  G
G  H  N  S  N  O  E  N  E  S  D  T
E  E  E  A  N  E  O  J  E  P  E  D
S  R  D  O  O  T  S  R  B  E  A  R
T  O  F  I  S  G  V  H  F  U  T  H
I  F  O  R  C  E  S  L  U  A  S  M
```

Secret Phrase

... " __ __ __   __ __ __ __ __ __   __ __ __ __   __ __

__ __ __   __ __ __ __ __   __ __ __ __ ."   – 1 Samuel 17:32

David and the Giant

Answers

Secret Phrase

. . . "Your servant will go and fight him."

~ 1 Samuel 17:32

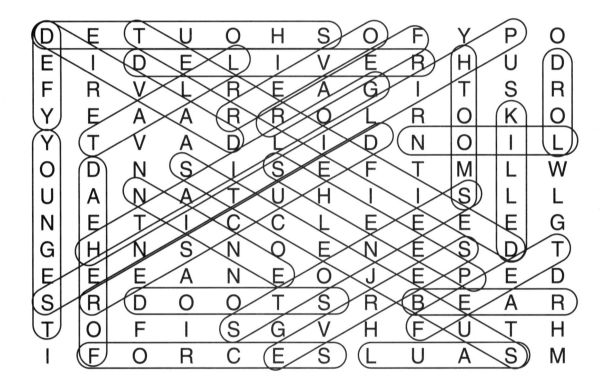

Example: Find PHILISTINES by counting across row 1 to column 11.

PHILISTINES (1,11) FORCES (13,2) GOLIATH (3,8) OVER (1,8) NINE (7,3) FEET (12,9)

TALL (5,2) STOOD (11,7) SHOUTED (1,7) SUBJECTS (13,11) SERVE (9,10) DEFY (1,1)

SAUL (13,11) TERRIFIED (1,3) DAVID (5,5) YOUNGEST (5,1) SHEEP (6,6) FEAR (1,9)

LION (5,12) BEAR (11,9) RESCUED (11,2) LORD (5,12) DELIVER (2,3) SMOOTH (7,10)

STONES (12,5) FOREHEAD (13,2) KILLED (4,11)

A Beautiful Temple
1 Kings 5

The Israelites wandered 40 years in the wilderness. During that time, the temple of God was a tent. After the people entered the Promised Land, they wanted to build a permanent temple. God gave King Solomon, the son of King David, the honor of building this temple. Solomon built a beautiful temple. In the secret phrase below, Jesus speaks of a different temple: His body.

HIRAM	BUILD	RULE	LABORERS
KING	ORDERS	GREAT	QUARRY
TYRE	CEDARS	NATION	BLOCKS
SOLOMON	LEBANON	WISDOM	DRESSED
ANOINTED	TIMBER	PROMISED	STONE
ENVOYS	PLEASED	CONSCRIPTED	TEMPLE

```
D  E  S  D  R  E  S  S  E  D  T  R  T
O  Y  S  R  E  D  R  O  Y  E  T  E  H
S  Y  O  V  N  E  I  R  S  T  M  L  T
C  E  D  A  R  S  R  S  E  P  M  E  P
L  E  L  G  D  A  R  D  L  I  U  B  W
A  N  N  U  U  E  N  E  D  R  I  A  I
S  I  R  Q  R  L  S  O  W  C  I  N  S
K  L  E  O  L  P  N  I  I  S  R  O  D
C  T  B  H  I  R  A  M  M  N  L  N  O
O  A  M  A  I  S  T  E  N  O  T  S  M
L  E  I  E  I  T  I  Y  M  C  R  E  A
B  R  T  G  ·  A  I  O  O  R  N  I  D
N  G  T  H  R  E  N  E  D  E  A  Y  S
```

Secret Phrase

... " _ _ _ _ _ _ _ _ _ _   _ _ _ _   _ _ _ _ _ _ _

_ _ _ _   _ _   _ _ _ _ _   _ _ _ _ _   _ _

_ _ _ _ _ _   _ _   _ _ _ _ _ _   _ _ _ _ _ ."

- John 2:19

A Beautiful Temple

Answers

Secret Phrase

. . . "Destroy this temple and I will raise it again in three days."

~ John 2:19

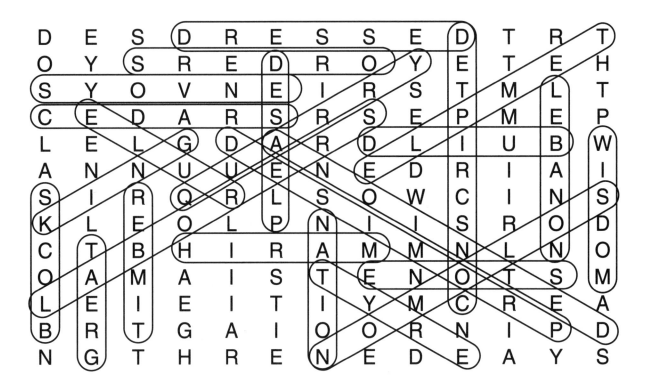

Example: Find HIRAM by counting down 9 rows and then across 4 columns.

HIRAM (9,4)   KING (8,1)   TYRE (10,7)   SOLOMON (7,13)   ANOINTED (5,6)

ENVOYS (3,6)   BUILD (5,12)   ORDERS (2,8)   CEDARS (4,1)   LEBANON (3,12)

TIMBER (12,3)   PLEASED (8,6)   RULE (7,5)   GREAT (13,2)   NATION (8,7)

WISDOM (5,13)   PROMISED (12,12)   CONSCRIPTED (11,10)   LABORERS (11,1)

QUARRY (7,4)   BLOCKS (12,1)   DRESSED (1,4)   STONE (10,12)   TEMPLE (1,13)

Elijah and the Widow's Son
1 Kings 17:7-24

Out of kindness, a poor widow gave Elijah some water and food. God rewarded her with a miracle: She never ran out of flour for making bread, and her jug of oil never ran empty. Later, her son died, but Elijah called upon the Lord to raise the boy back to life. Write the unused letters in the secret phrase to learn what the widow said about Elijah.

BROOK	STICKS	REPLIED	TRAGEDY	MOTHER
DRIED	BRING	HANDFUL	SICKNESS	
RAIN	WATER	FLOUR	STRETCHED	
LAND	DRINK	ELIJAH	RETURNED	
WIDOW	PIECE	SMALL	LIVED	
GATHERING	BREAD	CAKE	CARRIED	

```
N  O  S  S  K  C  I  T  S  W  I  F
K  N  O  S  T  N  W  S  M  A  L  L
G  A  T  H  E  R  I  N  G  R  A  O
T  G  R  A  I  N  E  R  E  N  H  U
A  T  N  J  L  Y  K  T  D  E  D  R
W  D  O  I  U  A  U  C  C  E  Y  H
W  A  V  L  R  R  R  E  I  H  D  A
I  E  T  E  N  B  I  L  B  S  E  N
D  R  I  E  D  P  P  E  R  A  G  D
O  B  D  M  R  E  H  T  O  M  A  F
W  C  A  R  R  I  E  D  O  A  R  U
N  O  F  G  O  D  C  A  K  E  T  L
```

Secret Phrase

... "___ ___ __ ___ ___ ___ ___ ___

___ ___ __ ___ ___ ___ _____." ...   – 1 Kings 17:24

Elijah and the Widow's Son

Answers

Secret Phrase

. . . "Now I know that you are a man of God." . . .

~ 1 Kings 17:24

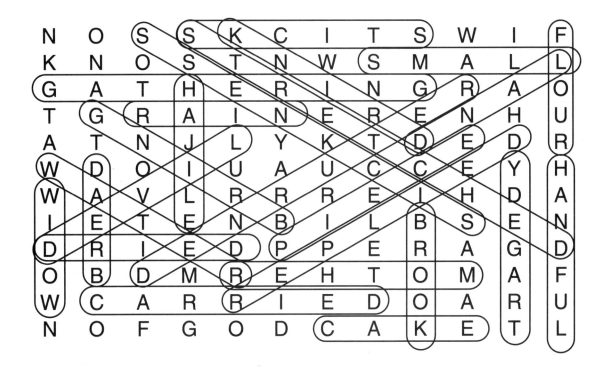

Example: Find BROOK by counting down 8 rows and then across 9 columns.

BROOK (8,9) DRIED (9,1) RAIN (4,3) LAND (2,12) WIDOW (7,1) GATHERING (3,1)

STICKS (1,9) BRING (8,6) WATER (6,1) DRINK (5,9) PIECE (9,6) BREAD (10,2)

REPLIED (11,5) HANDFUL (6,12) FLOUR (1,12) ELIJAH (8,4) SMALL (2,8)

CAKE (12,7) TRAGEDY (12,11) SICKNESS (8,10) STRETCHED (1,4)

RETURNED (3,10) LIVED (5,5) CARRIED (11,2) MOTHER (10,10)

Naaman Is Made Well
2 Kings 5:1-14

Leprosy was a greatly feared disease in Bible times because there was no cure. No one could touch lepers, so the lepers led lonely lives. When Naaman got the disease, he thought his life was over. But a young girl from Israel suggested he see Elisha, a prophet of God. Discover what Jesus said about Naaman by filling in the secret phrase.

NAAMAN	SOLDIER	KING	SEVEN	DIPPED
COMMANDER	LEPROSY	ELISHA	TIMES	HIMSELF
ARMY	YOUNG	ISRAEL	JORDAN	FLESH
HIGHLY	GIRL	CHARIOTS	WENT	RESTORED
REGARDED	MISTRESS	MESSENGER	AWAY	CLEAN
VALIANT	CURE	WASH	ANGRY	

```
J O R D A N Y K C N L Y O
T O C H A R I O T S R L N
R E C O M F N M T U E I H
E E A M G M Y S I N G G W
A A G T A M S D E H G I C
N L E N R F L E S M I H A
R N D A E O S A M N I F E
D E O I S S W I N A L T N
R L G L T I S R A E L L D
A I Y A O T N E S L V I A
N S A V R M T H M C P E A
G H N E E D T N H P U S
R A S S D Y E R E I A N
Y S O R P E L D A W A Y E
```

Secret Phrase

…" ____ ____ __ _____ ____

_____ - _____ _____

____ _____." **– Luke 4:27**

43

Naaman Is Made Well

Answers

Secret Phrase

. . . "Not one of them was cleansed–only Naaman the Syrian."

~ Luke 4:27

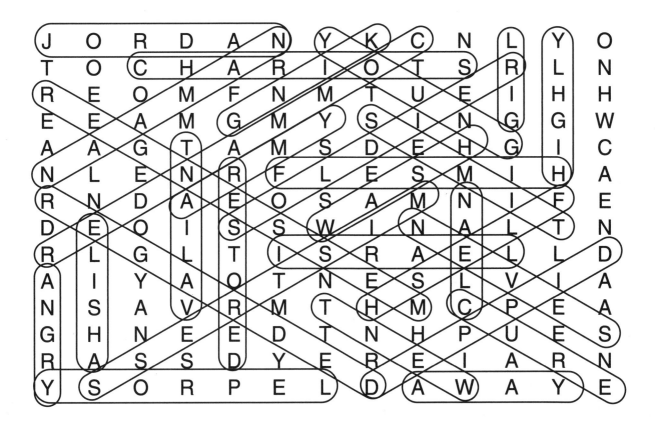

Example: Find NAAMAN by counting down 6 rows and then beginning in the first column.

NAAMAN (6,1) COMMANDER (1,9) ARMY (7,4) HIGHLY (6,12) REGARDED (7,1)

VALIANT (11,4) SOLDIER (8,5) LEPROSY (14,7) YOUNG (1,7) GIRL (4,11)

MISTRESS (7,9) CURE (11,10) KING (1,8) ELISHA (8,2) ISRAEL (9,6) CHARIOTS (2,3)

MESSENGER (11,9) WASH (8,7) SEVEN (12,13) TIMES (8,12) JORDAN (1,1)

WENT (14,10) AWAY (14,9) ANGRY (10,1) DIPPED (9,13) HIMSELF (6,12)

FLESH (7,12) RESTORED (6,5) CLEAN (11,10)

David's Beautiful Song
Psalm 23

Psalm 23 is one of the most beautiful songs ever written. It contains 119 words and can be read aloud in about 30 seconds. Yet this short passage is a powerful expression of God's love. If you have not already done so, memorize this psalm as you work the puzzle. Use the key words to help you recall the verses that you cannot remember in detail. In the secret phrase, Jesus uses words from Psalm 23 to describe Himself.

LORD	WATERS	VALLEY	PRESENCE	LOVE
SHEPHERD	RESTORES	SHADOW	ENEMIES	FOLLOW
GREEN	SOUL	DEATH	ANOINT	DAYS
PASTURES	GUIDES	STAFF	HEAD	LIFE
BESIDE	PATHS	COMFORT	SURELY	DWELL
QUIET	WALK	TABLE	GOODNESS	HOUSE

```
I  S  E  D  I  U  G  C  A  S  M  T
H  T  F  O  L  L  O  W  H  Y  H  E
W  A  L  K  D  M  O  A  Y  A  T  G
O  F  O  A  F  D  D  N  L  D  A  S
S  F  E  O  R  O  N  O  E  D  E  H
T  H  R  C  W  E  E  I  R  R  D  E
A  T  H  E  N  E  S  N  U  O  S  P
B  E  S  I  D  E  S  T  S  L  E  H
L  G  P  H  T  D  S  U  O  H  I  E
E  S  R  E  T  A  W  E  O  R  M  R
E  R  I  E  P  A  V  E  R  H  E  D
L  U  O  S  E  O  P  D  L  P  N  S
Q  E  F  I  L  N  V  A  L  L  E  Y
```

Secret Phrase

" __ ___ ____ _____

_____." . . .   – John 10:14

45

David's Beautiful Song

Answers

Secret Phrase

"I am the good shepherd." . . .

~ John 10:14

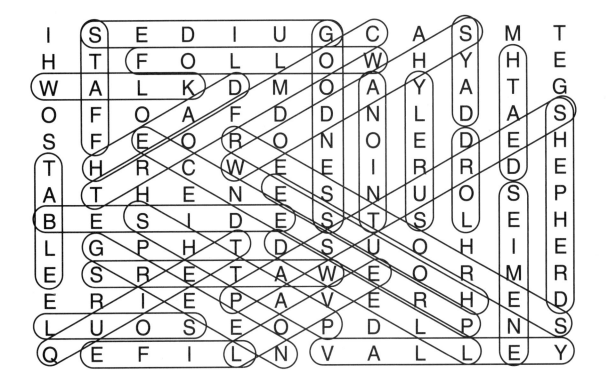

Example: Find LORD by counting down 8 rows and then across 10 columns.

LORD (8,10) SHEPHERD (4,12) GREEN (9,2) PASTURES (11,5) BESIDE (8,1)

QUIET (13,1) WATERS (10,7) RESTORES (5,5) SOUL (12,4) GUIDES (1,7)

PATHS (12,7) WALK (3,1) VALLEY (13,7) SHADOW (1,10) DEATH (6,11)

STAFF (1,2) COMFORT (1,8) TABLE (6,1) PRESENCE (12,10) ENEMIES (13,11)

ANOINT (3,8) HEAD (6,2) SURELY (8,9) GOODNESS (1,7) LOVE (13,5)

FOLLOW (2,3) DAYS (4,10) LIFE (13,5) DWELL (9,6) HOUSE (11,10)

The Fiery Furnace
Daniel 3:19-30

While in captivity in Babylon, three young Israelites refused to bow down before the country's false god. The king was furious and threw the men into a furnace. He expected them to die. Instead, the faithful young men came out unharmed. Solve the secret phrase to learn the choice that all children of God must make.

SHADRACH   BLAZING   UNHARMED   ANGEL

MESHACH   FURNACE   FORTH   RESCUED

ABEDNEGO   AMAZEMENT   HAIR   PROMOTED

SEVEN   FOUR   HEADS   PROVINCE

TIMES   WALKING   SINGED   BABYLON

THROW   UNBOUND   PRAISE

```
W  D  E  M  U  S  T  O  B  P  F  W
E  Y  E  C  N  I  V  O  R  P  O  G
O  D  R  U  O  E  C  A  N  R  U  F
S  A  H  T  C  G  I  S  H  O  R  H
W  H  C  D  E  S  E  T  U  M  N  R
A  M  A  Z  E  M  E  N  T  O  O  G
L  H  H  D  I  G  H  R  D  T  L  N
K  E  S  T  R  A  N  A  T  E  Y  I
I  A  E  H  R  A  N  I  I  D  B  Z
N  D  M  M  A  O  C  G  S  R  A  A
G  S  E  V  E  N  F  H  E  N  B  L
M  D  N  U  O  B  N  U  E  L  N  B
```

Secret Phrase

... " __ __ __ __ __ __ __ __ __ __ __ __ __ __

__ __ __ __ __ __ __ __ __ __ __ __ __ __ __ __ !" – Acts 5:29

The Fiery Furnace

Answers

Secret Phrase

. . . "We must obey God rather than men!"

~ Acts 5:29

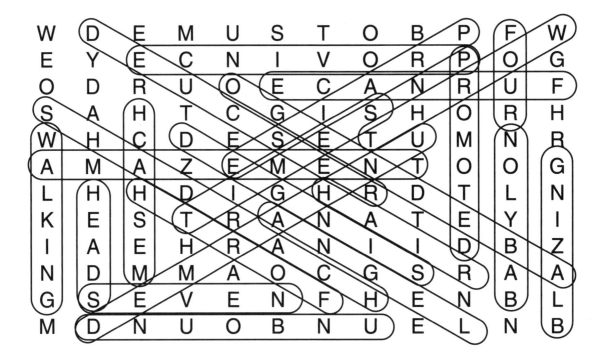

Example: Find SHADRACH by counting down 4 rows and then beginning in the first column.

SHADRACH (4,1) MESHACH (10,3) ABEDNEGO (10,12) SEVEN (11,2) TIMES (8,4)

THROW (5,8) BLAZING (12,12) FURNACE (3,12) AMAZEMENT (6,1) FOUR (1,11)

WALKING (5,1) UNBOUND (12,8) UNHARMED (5,9) FORTH (11,7) HAIR (7,7)

HEADS (7,2) SINGED (10,9) PRAISE (1,10) ANGEL (8,6) RESCUED (7,8)

PROMOTED (2,10) PROVINCE (2,10) BABYLON (11,11)

The Lions' Den
Daniel 6

Although in captivity in Babylon, Daniel had become one of the king's favorite advisers. But Daniel's enemies found him praying to God rather than to the king. Daniel was thrown into a lions' den to be killed. He prayed to God all night, and he was not afraid. Guess who was overjoyed to find Daniel alive the next morning? The king! Solve the secret phrase to find out what Jesus said about death in His name.

DANIEL	NEITHER	WRITING	LIONS	INNOCENT
EXCEPTIONAL	CORRUPT	UPSTAIRS	LIGHT	OVERJOYED
QUALITIES	ISSUE	KNEES	DAWN	FEAR
WHOLE	EDICT	PRAYED	ANGEL	REVERENCE
KINGDOM	DARIUS	ORDER	SHUT	
TRUSTWORTHY	DECREE	THREW	MOUTHS	

```
D  L  I  Q  D  S  H  T  U  O  M  O  L
A  E  N  S  U  D  E  Y  A  R  P  I  A
W  I  Y  I  S  A  N  G  E  L  G  O  N
N  N  R  O  T  U  L  V  B  H  E  A  O
E  A  F  R  J  N  E  I  T  H  E  R  I
D  D  Y  H  T  R  O  W  T  S  U  R  T
I  O  R  D  E  R  E  N  A  I  D  U  P
C  S  E  N  I  R  E  V  M  C  E  P  E
T  E  C  L  H  C  D  O  O  F  C  S  C
T  E  H  T  O  O  S  R  D  S  R  T  X
E  N  W  N  F  H  R  H  G  O  E  A  E
K  K  N  E  U  U  W  I  N  L  E  I  L
T  I  A  T  P  S  N  O  I  L  H  R  E
W  R  I  T  I  N  G  B  K  O  D  S  Y
```

Secret Phrase

" __ __ __ __ __ __ __ __ __ __ __ __ __ __ __ __

__ __ __ __ __ __ __ __ __ __ __ __ __ __ __ __ __

__ __ __ __ __ ." . . .   **– Matthew 10:28**

49

The Lions' Den

Answers

Secret Phrase

"Do not be afraid of those who kill the body." . . .

~ Matthew 10:28

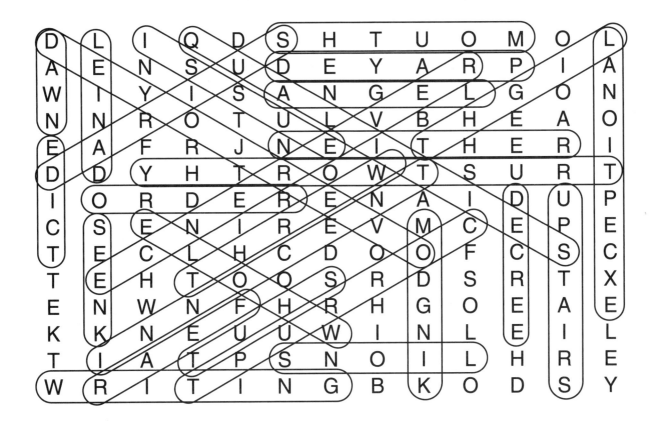

Example: Find DANIEL by counting down 6 rows and then across 2 columns.

DANIEL (6,2) EXCEPTIONAL (11,13) QUALITIES (1,4) WHOLE (12,7)

KINGDOM (14,9) TRUSTWORTHY (6,13) NEITHER (5,6) CORRUPT (8,10)

ISSUE (1,3) EDICT (5,1) DARIUS (6,1) DECREE (7,11) WRITING (14,1)

UPSTAIRS (7,12) KNEES (12,2) PRAYED (2,11) ORDER (7,2) THREW (10,4)

LIONS (13,10) LIGHT (1,13) DAWN (1,1) ANGEL (3,6) SHUT (10,7)

MOUTHS (1,11) INNOCENT (13,2) OVERJOYED (9,9) FEAR (11,5) REVERENCE (2,10)

Jonah in the Fish
Jonah 1-2

God commanded Jonah to preach to the people of Nineveh. Nineveh was a large city filled with wickedness. Rather than doing as God said, Jonah went in the opposite direction and boarded a ship. During a fierce storm, the sailors threw him overboard. A great fish swallowed him. Afterward, Jonah did preach to Nineveh, and the people repented. Solve the secret phrase to learn what Jesus says about Jonah — and about Himself!

JONAH	WIND	AFRAID	ROUGHER	BELLY
CITY	VIOLENT	DEEP	THREW	THREE
NINEVEH	STORM	SLEEP	OVERBOARD	DAYS
WICKEDNESS	SHIP	CAST	GREAT	NIGHTS
JOPPA	BREAK	LOTS	FISH	PRAYED
TARSHISH	SAILORS	CALAMITY	SWALLOW	

```
T  H  R  E  E  N  O  W  P  I  H  S
H  S  R  O  U  G  H  E  R  O  L  F
R  S  A  N  V  D  H  E  G  E  I  R
E  W  I  C  K  E  D  N  E  S  S  A
W  E  A  H  V  Y  R  P  H  C  P  T
E  I  R  E  S  A  M  B  A  P  T  H
J  V  N  A  R  R  T  L  O  T  S  B
O  I  Y  D  O  P  A  J  D  A  R  N
N  O  J  T  L  M  E  T  O  E  R  B
A  L  S  D  I  A  R  F  A  N  E  D
H  E  A  T  A  C  G  K  H  L  I  P
S  N  Y  H  S  W  A  L  L  O  W  E
S  T  H  G  I  N  S  Y  A  D  R  E
```

Secret Phrase

" ... _____ _____ _____ _____

_____ ___ _____ ."   – Matthew 12:41

51

Jonah in the Fish

Answers

Secret Phrase

"... Now one greater than Jonah is here."

~ Matthew 12:41

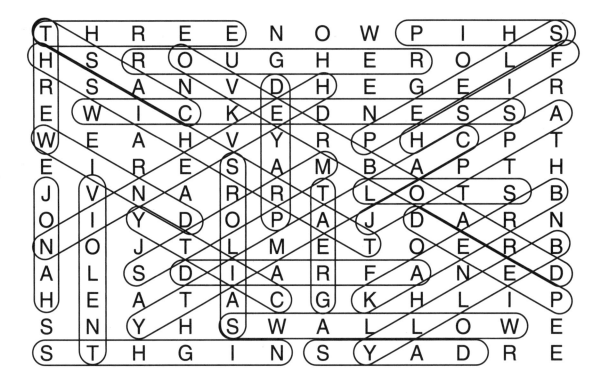

Example: Find JONAH by counting down 7 rows and then beginning in the first column.

JONAH (7,1) CITY (11,6) NINEVEH (9,1) WICKEDNESS (4,2) JOPPA (8,8)

TARSHISH (9,8) WIND (5,1) VIOLENT (7,2) STORM (10,3) SHIP (1,12)

BREAK (7,12) SAILORS (12,5) AFRAID (10,9) DEEP (8,9) SLEEP (1,12)

CAST (4,4)   LOTS (7,8) CALAMITY (5,10) ROUGHER (2,3) THREW (1,1)

OVERBOARD (2,4) GREAT (11,7) FISH (2,12) SWALLOW (12,5) BELLY (9,12)

THREE (1,1)   DAYS (13,10) NIGHTS (13,6) PRAYED (8,6)

The Angel Visits Mary
Luke 1:26-38

The angel Gabriel visited Mary, a young Jewish girl. His message told of an awesome responsibility. God had chosen Mary to be the mother of Jesus. Her reply showed her obedient heart. "I am the Lord's servant," Mary answered. "May it be to me as you have said." Mary raised Jesus as God's Son. Later, she was present during an important event in Jesus' life – His crucifixion. Solve the secret phrase to learn if Jesus saw His mother.

GABRIEL	HIGHLY	NAME	KINGDOM	IMPOSSIBLE
VIRGIN	FAVORED	JESUS	HOLY	SERVANT
JOSEPH	WONDERED	GREAT	GHOST	ACCORDING
MARY	ANGEL	THRONE	SPIRIT	ANSWERED
GREETINGS	SAID	DAVID	BORN	
WOMEN	CHILD	REIGN	NOTHING	

```
J  S  U  S  E  J  N  E  M  O  W  E
D  Y  P  G  G  N  I  H  T  O  N  S
U  I  L  I  R  L  S  S  N  A  M  E
F  A  V  O  R  E  D  D  I  A  S  E
G  A  B  A  H  I  E  C  H  I  L  D
H  N  N  A  D  R  T  T  M  B  E  W
O  S  I  H  E  B  M  O  I  N  H  A
S  W  G  D  I  A  D  S  O  N  N  J
T  E  R  I  R  G  S  R  S  G  G  O
M  R  I  Y  N  O  H  O  E  I  R  S
T  E  V  I  P  T  C  L  H  E  E  E
E  D  K  M  R  T  H  C  Y  R  A  P
E  R  I  E  S  E  R  V  A  N  T  H
```

Secret Phrase

... _ _ _ _ _   _ _ _   _ _ _   _ _ _ _ _

_ _ _ _ _ _ _ .... – John 19:26

53

The Angel Visits Mary

Answers

Secret Phrase

. . . Jesus saw his mother there. . . .

~ John 19:26

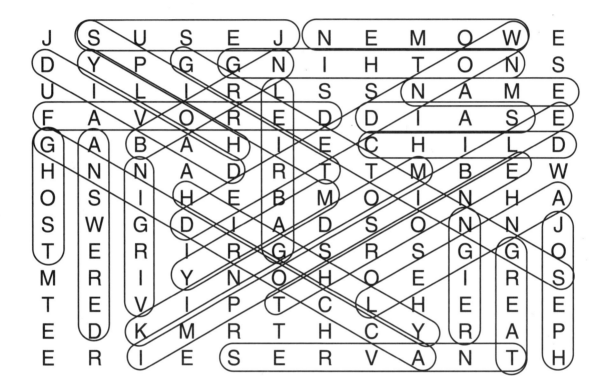

Example: Find GABRIEL by counting down 9 rows and then across 6 columns.

GABRIEL (9,6) VIRGIN (11,3) JOSEPH (8,12) MARY (7,7) GREETINGS (2,4)

WOMEN (1,11) HIGHLY (7,4) FAVORED (4,1) WONDERED (1,11) ANGEL (7,12)

SAID (4,11) CHILD (5,8) NAME (3,9) JESUS (1,6) GREAT (9,11) THRONE (11,6)

DAVID (6,5) REIGN (12,10) KINGDOM (12,3) HOLY (5,5) GHOST (5,1)

SPIRIT (1,2) BORN (5,3) NOTHING (2,11) IMPOSSIBLE (13,3) SERVANT (13,5)

ACCORDING (13,9) ANSWERED (5,2)

The Shepherds Hear About Jesus
Luke 2:8-20

During Bible times, shepherds were viewed as humble people. However, God chose to announce the birth of His Son to them. After seeing the baby Jesus, the shepherds told others that the Savior of the world had been born. Solve the secret phrase to learn why the shepherds could be called "beautiful."

▬ ▬

SHEPHERDS	NIGHT	MANGER	RESTS	PRAISING
LIVING	ANGEL	GLORY	BETHLEHEM	
FIELDS	NEWS	HIGHEST	MARY	
KEEPING	SAVIOR	EARTH	JOSEPH	
WATCH	WRAPPED	PEACE	BABY	
FLOCKS	CLOTHS	FAVOR	RETURNED	

▬ ▬

```
H  W  F  Y  R  O  L  G  B  A  B  Y
O  M  A  N  G  E  R  E  W  B  T  E
S  A  V  T  U  G  T  T  I  F  H  A
A  D  O  H  C  H  N  U  U  T  G  N
V  L  R  P  L  H  A  I  R  G  I  G
I  F  I  E  L  D  S  A  V  N  N  E
O  R  H  S  H  E  E  T  H  I  E  L
R  E  I  O  O  P  S  P  P  S  L  D
M  E  G  J  W  P  E  E  P  I  H  O
B  R  H  N  I  N  E  H  M  A  R  Y
G  G  E  O  O  K  D  A  S  R  R  N
E  W  S  K  C  O  L  F  C  P  W  W
S  H  T  O  L  C  S  T  S  E  R  S
```

Secret Phrase

…" __ __ __ __ __ __ __ __ __ __ __ __ __ __ __ __ __…

__ __ __ __ __ __ __ __ __ __ __ __ __ __ __ __ __ __ __

__ __ __ __ __ !"   – Romans 10:15

55

The Shepherds Hear About Jesus

Answers

Secret Phrase

. . . "How beautiful are...those who bring good news!"

~ Romans 10:15

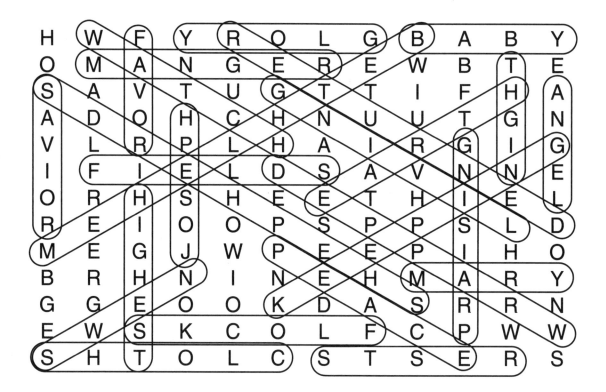

Example: Find SHEPHERDS by counting down 11 rows and then across 9 columns.

SHEPHERDS (11,9) LIVING (8,11) FIELDS (6,2) KEEPING (11,6) WATCH (1,2)

FLOCKS (12,8) NIGHT (6,11) ANGEL (3,12) NEWS (10,4) SAVIOR (3,1)

WRAPPED (12,12) CLOTHS (13,6) MANGER (2,2) GLORY (1,8) HIGHEST (7,3)

EARTH (7,7) PEACE (9,6) FAVOR (1,3) RESTS (13,11) BETHLEHEM (1,9)

MARY (10,9) JOSEPH (9,4) BABY (1,9) RETURNED (1,5) PRAISING (12,10)

Wise Men Worship Jesus
Matthew 2:1-12

A star guided the wise men, known as Magi, a long distance so they could worship the baby Jesus. They gave Him three different types of gifts. Can you name the three gifts? (See the search words.) The secret phrase reveals the city where Old Testament prophets said Jesus would be born.

MAGI   DISTURBED   SHEPHERD   OPENED   MYRRH

STAR   CHRIST   ISRAEL   TREASURES

EAST   BORN   CHILD   PRESENTED

KING   BETHLEHEM   WORSHIP   GIFTS

HEROD   JUDEA   OVERJOYED   GOLD

HEARD   RULER   EXCEEDING   INCENSE

```
D  B  E  S  H  E  P  H  E  R  D  E  T
R  I  L  E  A  R  S  I  H  E  L  X  E
A  H  S  P  S  E  M  N  Y  O  U  C  B
E  A  S  T  R  S  D  O  E  T  O  E  F
H  S  F  Y  U  E  J  L  O  C  T  E  U
W  I  T  I  L  R  S  L  O  H  N  D  L
G  P  C  A  E  U  B  E  L  G  J  I  O
D  M  I  V  R  S  E  E  N  F  U  N  O
L  R  O  H  H  A  H  I  D  T  D  G  M
I  G  A  M  S  E  K  D  E  N  E  P  O
H  R  R  Y  M  R  R  E  R  O  A  D  N
C  H  R  I  S  T  O  O  E  W  H  O  W
I  L  L  B  E  R  B  W  D  U  L  E  R
```

Secret Phrase

"... _ _ _ _ _ _ _ _ _ _ _ , ... _ _ _ _ _ _ _ _ _

_ _ _ _ _ _ _ _ _ _ _ _ _ _ _ _

_ _ _ _ _ _ _ _ _ _ _ _ _ _ _ _ _ _ ." ...   – Micah 5:2

Wise Men Worship Jesus

Answers

Secret Phrase

"... Bethlehem, ... out of you will come for me one who will be ruler." ...

~ Micah 5:2

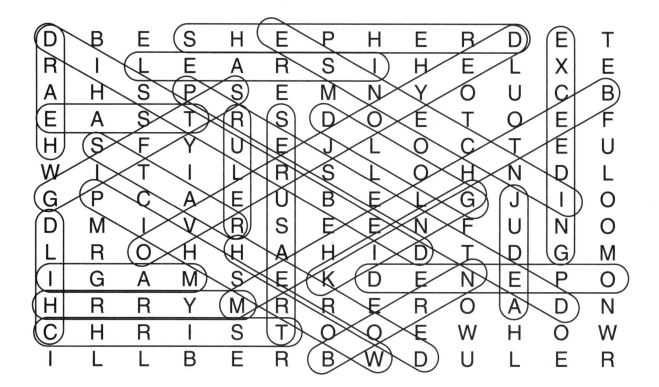

Example: Find MAGI by counting down 10 rows and then across 4 columns.

MAGI (10,4) STAR (5,2) EAST (4,1) KING (10,7) HEROD (9,5) HEARD (5,1)

DISTURBED (1,1) CHRIST (12,1) BORN (13,7) BETHLEHEM (3,13) JUDEA (7,11)

RULER (4,5) SHEPHERD (1,4) ISRAEL (2,8) CHILD (12,1) WORSHIP (13,8)

OVERJOYED (9,3) EXCEEDING (1,12) OPENED (10,13) TREASURES (12,6)

PRESENTED (3,4) GIFTS (7,1) GOLD (7,10) INCENSE (7,12) MYRRH (11,5)

Jesus as a Boy in the Temple
Luke 2:41-52

The book of Luke reports how Jesus became separated from His family when He was 12 years old. His mother and father looked everywhere for Him. They checked with friends and relatives, but He was not with them. Then they found Him at the temple! After you discover the search words in the grid, the unused letters will tell why God sent His Son to earth.

JERUSALEM	LOOKING	TEACHERS	MOTHER	WISDOM
TWELVE	RELATIVES	LISTENING	FATHERS	STATURE
YEARS	WENT	ASKING	HOUSE	FAVOR
FEAST	BACK	QUESTIONS	NAZARETH	
CUSTOM	FOUND	ANSWERS	JESUS	
COMPANY	TEMPLE	ASTONISHED	GREW	

```
T  H  E  J  F  T  T  E  M  P  L  E
F  A  S  R  E  W  S  N  A  T  H  S
F  A  T  H  E  R  S  A  S  E  T  U
S  R  V  L  Y  H  U  N  E  A  E  O
T  E  V  O  S  E  O  S  S  F  A  H
A  E  V  E  R  I  A  N  A  T  C  H
T  J  I  I  T  T  M  R  L  L  H  S
U  E  A  S  T  O  N  I  S  H  E  D
R  S  E  S  D  A  S  E  R  T  R  M
E  U  D  S  K  T  L  E  W  E  S  O
Q  S  I  N  E  I  H  E  S  R  B  T
O  W  N  N  U  T  N  T  R  A  O  S
G  N  I  K  O  O  L  G  C  Z  B  U
E  N  S  M  A  V  F  K  I  A  O  C
G  R  E  W  C  O  M  P  A  N  Y  R
```

Secret Phrase

... ___ ___   ___ ___ ___ ___   ___ ___ ___   ___ ___ ___

___ ___ ___   ___ ___   ___   ___ ___ ... ___ ___ ___ ___ ...

- 1 John 4:14

Jesus as Boy in the Temple

Answers

Secret Phrase

. . . The Father has sent his son to be...Savior. . . .

~ 1 John 4:14

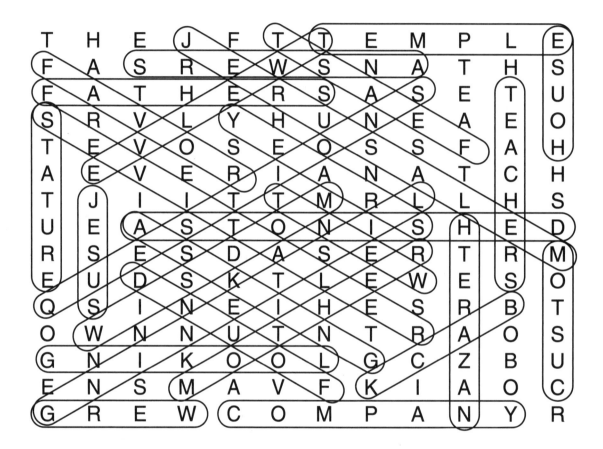

Example: Find Jerusalem by counting going to row 1 and counting to column 4.

JERUSALEM (1,4) TWELVE (1,7) YEARS (4,5) FEAST (5,10) CUSTOM (14,12)

COMPANY (15,5) LOOKING (13,7) RELATIVES (12,9) WENT (10,9) BACK (11,11)

FOUND (14,7) TEMPLE (1,7) TEACHERS (3,11) LISTENING (7,9) ASKING (8,3)

QUESTIONS (11,1) ANSWERS (2,9) ASTONISHED (8,3) MOTHER (14,4)

FATHERS (3,1) HOUSE (5,12) NAZARETH (15,10) JESUS (7,2) GREW (15,1)

WISDOM (12,2) STATURE (4,1) FAVOR (2,1)

Jesus Is Baptized
Matthew 3:13-17

People came from all around to hear John the Baptist preach and to be baptized by him in the Jordan River. Jesus also went to John the Baptist to be baptized. At first, some people mistakenly thought that John the Baptist was the Savior. Solve the secret phrase to read what John the Baptist said about himself.

▬ ▬

GALILEE	NEED	HEAVEN	VOICE
JORDAN	JESUS	OPENED	SAID
BAPTIZED	REPLIED	SPIRIT	WHOM
JOHN	PROPER	DESCENDING	LOVE
DETER	FULFILL	DOVE	WELL
SAYING	WATER	LIGHTING	PLEASED

▬ ▬

```
H  E  R  W  H  O  C  O  D  O  V  E
M  J  E  S  U  S  L  L  E  W  E  C
S  D  T  S  A  Y  I  N  G  A  D  I
D  E  E  N  F  G  D  E  N  E  P  O
T  S  D  Z  H  M  A  E  I  R  D  V
R  C  P  T  I  M  O  L  E  F  E  P
H  E  I  I  A  T  P  H  I  U  S  R
S  N  T  S  R  E  P  E  W  L  A  O
G  D  A  A  I  E  A  S  F  E  P
U  I  R  P  W  A  T  V  B  I  L  E
D  N  A  D  R  O  J  E  O  L  P  R
S  G  S  E  J  O  H  N  D  L  M  E
```

Secret Phrase

... " __ __ __ __ __ __ __ __ __ __ __ __ __ __ __ __ __ __ __ __ __

__ __ __ __ __ __ __ __ __ __ __ __ __ __ __ __ __." ...   **– John 1:15**

Jesus Is Baptized

Answers

Secret Phrase

. . . "He who comes after me has surpassed me." . . .

~ John 1:15

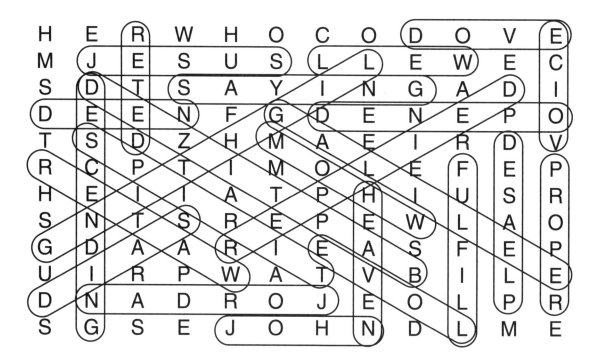

Example: Find GALILEE by counting down 4 rows and then across 6 columns.

GALILEE (4,6) JORDAN (11,7) BAPTIZED (10,9) JOHN (12,5) DETER (5,3)

SAYING (3,4) NEED (4,4) JESUS (2,2) REPLIED (9,5) PROPER (6,12)

FULFILL (6,10) WATER (10,5) HEAVEN (7,8) OPENED (4,12) SPIRIT (5,2)

DESCENDING (3,2) DOVE (1,9) LIGHTING (2,8) VOICE (5,12) SAID (8,4)

WHOM (8,9) LOVE (12,10) WELL (2,10) PLEASED (11,11)

The Apostles
Mark 3:13-19; Acts 1:26; Titus 1:1

Can you name the original 12 apostles whom Jesus chose? Use the search words below as a guide. The apostles included two sets of brothers: James and John, and Peter and Andrew. The Bible says that Herod put James to death, and then he threw Peter in prison. Write the unused letters in the blanks to see what Jesus said would happen to His apostles.

APPOINTED	BROTHER	BARTHOLOMEW	JUDAS	APOSTLE
TWELVE	JOHN	MATTHEW	ISCARIOT	
SIMON	BOANERGES	THOMAS	BETRAYED	
PETER	THUNDER	ALPHAEUS	MATTHIAS	
JAMES	ANDREW	THADDAEUS	PAUL	
ZEBEDEE	PHILIP	ZEALOT	SERVANT	

```
B  R  O  T  H  E  R  S  O  M  P  S
A  A  E  O  F  W  H  O  M  E  T  A
R  P  N  S  H  E  Y  W  T  I  L  M
T  O  P  D  E  E  D  E  B  E  Z  O
H  S  L  O  R  M  R  O  K  D  I  H
O  T  S  L  I  E  A  L  A  E  N  T
L  L  D  U  O  N  W  J  P  Y  N  T
O  E  H  E  E  E  T  H  R  A  S  I
M  T  H  R  V  A  I  E  V  R  J  S
E  W  G  E  Y  L  D  R  D  T  U  C
W  E  W  I  I  J  E  D  L  E  D  A
S  H  L  P  P  S  O  W  A  B  A  R
I  T  R  E  D  N  U  H  T  H  S  I
M  T  E  L  U  A  P  R  N  S  T  O
O  A  E  T  O  L  A  E  Z  C  U  T
N  M  T  M  A  T  T  H  I  A  S  E
```

Secret Phrase

..."___ ___ ___ ___ ___ ___

___ ___ ___ ___ ___

___ ___ ___,"   – Luke 11:49

The Apostles

Answers

Secret Phrase

. . . "Some of whom they will kill and others they will persecute."

~ Luke 11:49

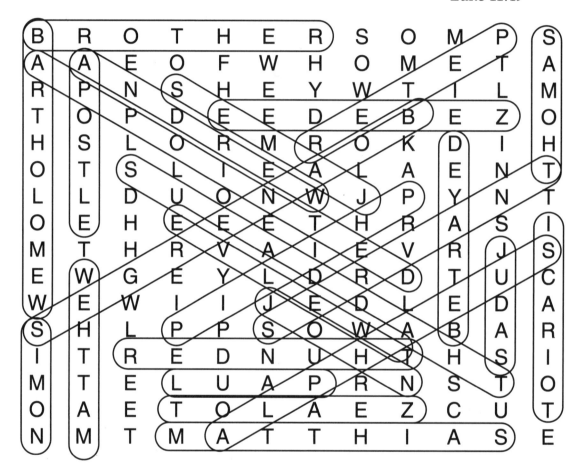

Example: Find APPOINTED by counting down 2 rows and then stop at the first column.

APPOINTED (2,1) TWELVE (13,9) SIMON (12,1) PETER (1,11) JAMES (7,8)

ZEBEDEE (4,11) BROTHER (1,1) JOHN (11,6) BOANERGES (4,9) THUNDER (13,9)

ANDREW (2,2) PHILIP (7,9) BARTHOLOMEW (1,1) MATTHEW (16,2)

THOMAS (6,12) ALPHAEUS (16,5) THADDAEUS (14,11) ZEALOT (15,9)

JUDAS (9,11) ISCARIOT (8,12) BETRAYED (12,10) MATTHIAS (16,4)

PAUL (14,7) SERVANT (12,6) APOSTLE (2,2)

Jesus Raises a Boy from the Dead
Luke 7:11-17

Jesus performed many miracles. Some He did to show His power so people would know He was the Messiah. But He also did miracles simply because He cared about people and felt compassion for them. In this story, Jesus felt the sorrow of a mother, so He restored her son back to life. In the secret phrase, find out what was one sign to the people that Jesus was indeed the Son of God.

NAIN	MOTHER	BEGAN	GREAT	JUDEA
DISCIPLES	WIDOW	TALK	PROPHET	COUNTRY
TOWN	LORD	GAVE	APPEARED	
GATE	HEART	FILLED	HELP	
DEAD	TOUCHED	PRAISED	PEOPLE	
CARRIED	YOUNG	GLORIFIED	NEWS	

```
H  E  L  P  T  F  I  L  L  E  D
H  T  D  S  P  R  O  P  H  E  T
N  A  G  E  B  N  E  D  S  D  C
N  G  J  L  R  E  I  I  T  A  A
E  Y  U  P  O  A  A  A  R  E  T
W  O  D  I  W  R  E  R  N  D  O
S  U  E  C  P  R  I  P  D  T  U
A  N  A  S  G  E  R  F  P  R  C
E  G  R  I  D  H  O  N  I  A  H
L  O  R  D  A  T  W  P  I  E  D
Y  R  T  N  U  O  C  S  L  H  D
E  K  L  A  T  M  G  A  V  E  D
```

Secret Phrase

... "___ ." ...

- Luke 7:22

Jesus Raises a Boy from the Dead

Answers

Secret Phrase

. . . "The dead are raised." . . .
~ Luke 7:22

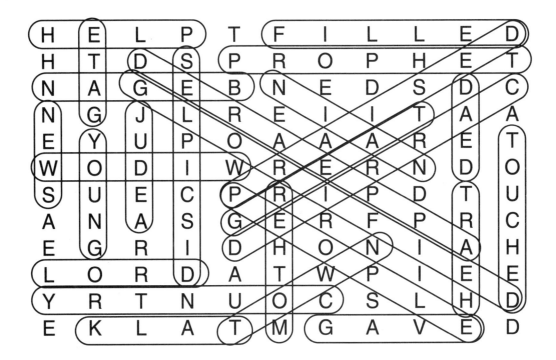

Example: Find NAIN by counting down 6 rows and then across 9 columns.

NAIN (6,9) DISCIPLES (10,4) TOWN (12,5) GATE (4,2) DEAD (6,10)

CARRIED (3,11) MOTHER (12,6) WIDOW (6,5) LORD (10,1) HEART (11,10)

TOUCHED (5,11) YOUNG (5,2) BEGAN (3,5) TALK (12,5) GAVE (12,7)

FILLED (1,6) PRAISED (7,5) GLORIFIED (3,3) GREAT (8,5) PROPHET (2,5)

APPEARED (9,10) HELP (1,1) PEOPLE (7,5) NEWS (4,1) JUDEA (4,3) COUNTRY (11,7)

Food for 5,000

Luke 9:10-17

Sometimes Jesus wanted to be alone with His disciples, but a great crowd often would follow Him to hear His teaching and receive healing. In this story, the crowd followed Jesus to a remote place where there was no food. Jesus fed 5,000 people using only five loaves and two fish. The secret phrase tells why He did this miracle.

AFTERNOON	COUNTRYSIDE	FISH	THANKS
TWELVE	FOOD	THOUSAND	BROKE
SEND	LODGING	GROUPS	SATISFIED
CROWD	REMOTE	FIFTY	PICKED
AWAY	FIVE	LOOKING	BASKETFULS
VILLAGES	LOAVES	HEAVEN	

```
S D E K C I P J E S V D
A L L O O K I N G Y I N
U F U S U S E V A O L A
S H T F N E H W A D L S
S E C E T H A N K S A U
P A N O R E B F C T G O
U V M D Y N K R I F E H
O E O T S M O S O S S T
R N F P I W F O A K H A
G I S S D I D I N B E I
F E V L E W T O V N O N
T L O D G I N G H E E M
```

Secret Phrase

. . . ___ ___ ___ ___ . . ___ ___ ___   ___ ___ ___ ___ ___ ___ ___ ___ ___

___ ___   ___ ___ ___ ___ ___ . . . .   **- Mark 6:34**

Food for 5,000

Answers

Secret Phrase

. . . Jesus…had compassion on them. . . .

~ Mark 6:34

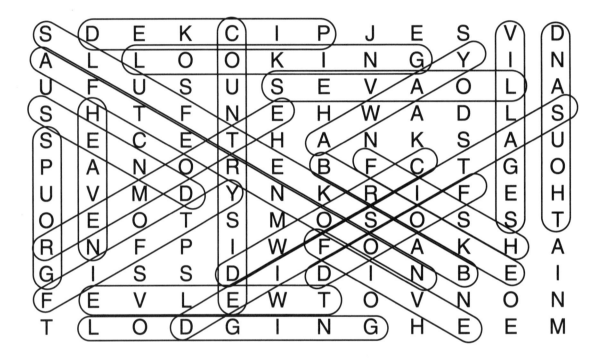

Example: Find AFTERNOON by counting down 2 rows and stopping at the first column.

AFTERNOON (2,1) TWELVE (11,7) SEND (4,1) CROWD (6,9) AWAY (5,7)

VILLAGES (1,11) COUNTRYSIDE (1,5) FOOD (7,10) LODGING (12,2)

REMOTE (9,1) FIVE (9,7) LOAVES (3,11) FISH (6,8) THOUSAND (8,12)

GROUPS (10,1) FIFTY (11,1) LOOKING (2,3) HEAVEN (4,2) THANKS (5,5)

BROKE (6,7) SATISFIED (4,12) PICKED (1,7) BASKETFULS (10,10)

Walking on Water
Matthew 14:22-33

The disciples were terrified when they saw an unexpected sight: Jesus walking on the water! One of the disciples (do you know which one?) stepped out of the boat to walk to Jesus, but the disciple doubted Jesus' power to aid him, and he began to sink. Jesus rescued him. After you find the words in the puzzle grid, write the unused letters in the blanks to spell out what Jesus said to calm the disciples' fears.

DISCIPLES	FOURTH	GHOST	AFRAID	FAITH
BOAT	WATCH	FEAR	SINK	WIND
HIMSELF	NIGHT	TAKE	SAVE	CLIMBED
PRAY	JESUS	COURAGE	REACHED	DIED
EVENING	WALKING	PETER	HAND	DOWN
ALONE	TERRIFIED	REPLIED	CAUGHT	

```
T  A  K  D  D  H  W  A  T  C  H  E
H  C  N  E  E  D  A  F  A  I  T  H
Y  I  K  V  I  O  L  N  I  G  H  T
W  A  M  A  L  U  K  R  D  A  E  R
T  S  R  S  P  G  I  G  E  R  P  U
C  F  E  P  E  I  N  E  R  E  T  O
A  S  E  L  R  L  G  I  T  I  B  F
U  I  U  A  P  A  F  E  N  O  L  A
G  N  S  S  R  I  R  I  A  E  D  O
H  K  D  U  E  N  C  T  T  B  V  D
T  E  O  D  A  J  T  S  O  H  G  E
F  C  W  R  D  E  B  M  I  L  C  I
A  I  N  R  E  A  C  H  E  D  D  D
```

Secret Phrase

. . . "___ ___ ___ ___ ___   ___ ___ ___ ___ ___ ___ ___! ___ ___   ___ ___   ___.

___ ___ ___ ___ ___ ,   ___ ___   ___ ___ ___ ___ ___ ___ ." — Mark 6:50

Walking on Water

Answers

Secret Phrase

. . . "Take courage! It is I. Don't be afraid."

~ Mark 6:50

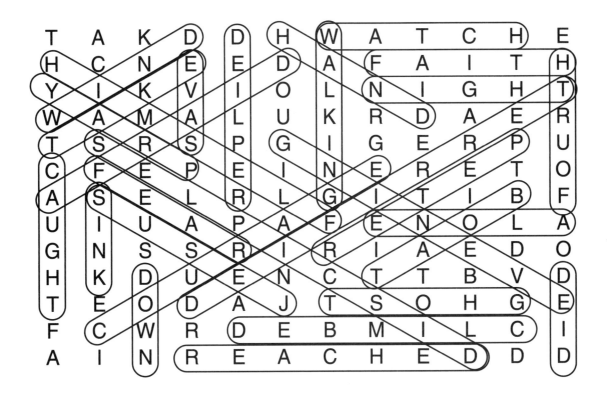

Example: Find DISCIPLES by counting down 13 rows and then across 10 columns.

DISCIPLES (13,10) BOAT (7,11) HIMSELF (2,1) PRAY (6,4) EVENING (11,12)

ALONE (8,12) FOURTH (7,12) WATCH (1,7) NIGHT (3,8) JESUS (11,6)

WALKING (1,7) TERRIFIED (3,12) GHOST (11,11) FEAR (6,2) TAKE (5,1)

COURAGE (12,2) PETER (5,11) REPLIED (7,5) AFRAID (7,1) SINK (7,2)

SAVE (5,4) REACHED (13,4) HAND (1,6) CAUGHT (6,1) FAITH (2,8)

WIND (4,1) CLIMBED (12,11) DIED (13,12) DOWN (10,3)

Paying the Tax
Matthew 17:24-27

Governments collect money – called "taxes" – from people who live in their territories. The money is used to build roads and bridges, operate schools and pay firefighters, police officers and other emergency workers. Even in Bible times, people had to pay taxes. In this story Jesus pays His tax, and He gets it straight from a fish's mouth! Solve the secret phrase to see what Jesus taught about taxes.

CAPERNAUM	SPEAK	TAKES	LINE	DRACHMA
COLLECTORS	SIMON	SONS	FIRST	COIN
PETER	WHOM	OTHERS	FISH	MONEY
TEACHER	KINGS	EXEMPT	OPEN	
TEMPLE	EARTH	OFFEND	MOUTH	
JESUS	DUTY	THROW	FIND	

```
G D N I F M O N E Y I
V E T J I O O K G O R
T A K E S D I U W E S
D H M S H N T T T A R
T R O U G E P E S H O
I N A S A M P M R N T
S S S C E N O P I O C
W R H X H H R L F M E
O E E Y W M N E O I L
R H G O T K A E N I L
H T R A E U D S P S O C
T O F F E N D N I O C
```

Secret Phrase

… " __ __ __ __ … __ __   __ __ __ __   __ __ __ __ __   __ __

__ __ __ ' __ ."   – Matthew 22:21

Paying the Tax

Answers

Secret Phrase

. . . "Give…to God what is God's."

~ Matthew 22:21

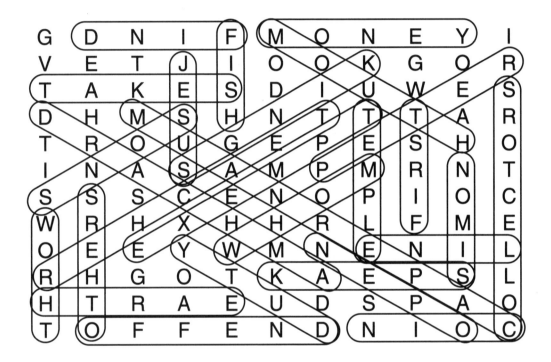

Example: Find CAPERNAUM by counting down 12 rows and then across 11 columns.

CAPERNAUM (12,11) COLLECTORS (12,11) PETER (6,7) TEACHER (4,7)

TEMPLE (4,8) JESUS (2,4) SPEAK (10,10) SIMON (10,10) WHOM (9,5)

KINGS (2,8) EARTH (11,5) DUTY (12,7) TAKES (3,1) SONS (4,4)

OTHERS (12,2) EXEMPT (9,3) OFFEND (12,2) THROW (12,1) LINE (9,11)

FIRST (8,9) FISH (1,5) OPEN (12,10) MOUTH (1,6) FIND (1,5) DRACHMA (4,1)

COIN (12,11) MONEY (1,6)

The Good Shepherd
Luke 10:1-21

Shepherds combined their flocks into a single pen at night. The next morning, they would call their sheep to come to them. The sheep understood which shepherd to follow because they knew their master's voice and trusted him. Shepherds took their sheep to pasture by walking in front of them. The sheep followed and did not have to be driven from behind. Solve the secret phrase to find out who is the "Great Shepherd."

▬ ▬

SHEEP	FIND	GOOD	FLOCK	RECEIVED
GATE	PASTURE	SHEPHERD	SCATTERS	FATHER
ROBBER	THIEF	HIRED	LOVES	POSSESSED
WATCHMAN	KILL	WOLF	DOWN	OPEN
KNOW	DESTROY	COMING	ACCORD	BLIND
VOICE	LIFE	ABANDONS	AUTHORITY	
SAVED	FULL	ATTACKS	COMMAND	

▬ ▬

```
J  V  E  S  D  N  I  L  B  U  S  T  H
F  A  O  E  R  E  C  E  I  V  E  D  T
L  U  R  I  O  G  V  R  E  G  E  N  G
K  I  L  L  C  D  A  A  N  S  T  A  A
H  W  F  L  C  E  R  I  S  H  T  M  B
S  S  A  E  A  H  M  E  F  E  T  M  A
E  R  E  T  P  O  S  A  H  E  H  O  N
H  E  E  V  C  S  T  R  D  P  I  C  D
Y  T  I  R  O  H  T  U  A  N  E  P  O
O  T  F  P  E  L  M  S  T  H  F  H  N
E  A  S  R  A  T  T  A  C  K  S  G  S
K  C  O  L  F  U  F  I  N  D  N  O  H
E  S  Y  O  R  T  S  E  D  F  L  O  W
E  P  R  E  B  B  O  R  N  W  O  D  W
```

Secret Phrase

· · · _ _ _ _ _ _ _ , _ _ _ _ _ _ _ _ _ _

_ _ _ _ _ _ _ _ _ _ _ _ _ _ _ _ _ _ _ _ .

The Good Shepherd

Answers

Secret Phrase

. . . Jesus, that great Shepherd of the sheep.

~ Hebrews 13:20

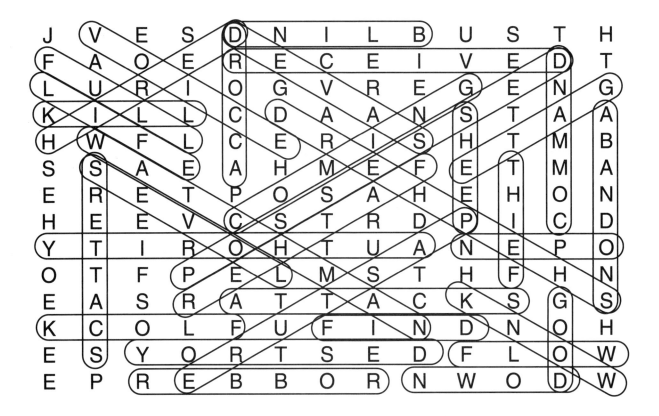

Example: Find SHEEP by counting down 4 rows and then across 10 columns.

SHEEP (4,10) GATE (3,13) ROBBER (14,8) WATCHMAN (5,2) KNOW (11,10)

VOICE (1,2) SAVED (5,9) FIND (12,7) PASTURE (8,10) THIEF (6,11) KILL (4,1)

DESTROY (13,9) LIFE (3,1) FULL (2,1) GOOD (11,12) SHEPHERD (11,13)

HIRED (5,1) WOLF (13,13) COMING (8,5) ABANDONS (4,13) ATTACKS (11,5)

FLOCK (12,5) SCATTERS (13,2) LOVES (10,6) DOWN (14,12) ACCORD (6,5)

AUTHORITY (9,9) COMMAND (8,12) RECEIVED (2,5) FATHER (6,9)

POSSESSED (10,4) OPEN (9,13) BLIND (1,9)

The Good Samaritan
Luke 10:25-37

Jesus knew that most Jews despised the Samaritans and would have nothing to do with them. The shortest way from Galilee to Judea was through Samaria, but Jews often would take a longer way rather than walk through Samaria. Jesus taught in this story that a good person can belong to any race. Solve the secret phrase to discover the question that Jesus answered with this powerful story.

OCCASION	HEART	JERUSALEM	HALF	BANDAGED
EXPERT	SOUL	JERICHO	DEAD	WOUNDS
ETERNAL	STRENGTH	ROBBERS	PRIEST	INNKEEPER
LIFE	MIND	STRIPPED	LEVITE	MERCY
LOVE	NEIGHBOR	CLOTHES	PASSED	
LORD	YOURSELF	LEAVING	SAMARITAN	

```
D  R  O  L  O  H  C  I  R  E  J  A
L  E  V  I  T  E  L  L  O  V  E  J
N  Y  D  F  S  O  O  T  B  W  H  E
S  O  O  E  E  C  T  R  H  I  D  R
D  R  S  U  I  C  H  E  G  M  E  U
N  F  E  Y  R  A  E  P  I  P  G  S
U  D  L  B  P  S  S  X  E  N  A  A
O  E  E  A  B  I  E  E  N  M  D  L
W  S  A  P  H  O  K  L  A  E  N  E
Y  S  V  I  P  N  R  R  F  D  A  M
C  A  I  D  N  I  I  G  A  H  B  B
R  P  N  I  S  T  R  E  N  G  T  H
E  I  G  O  A  R  D  T  R  A  E  H
M  L  A  N  R  E  T  E  S  O  U  L
```

Secret Phrase

... "____ ____ ____ ____ _____ ?"

– Luke 10:29

The Good Samaritan

Answers

Secret Phrase

. . . "And who is my neighbor?"

~ Luke 10:29

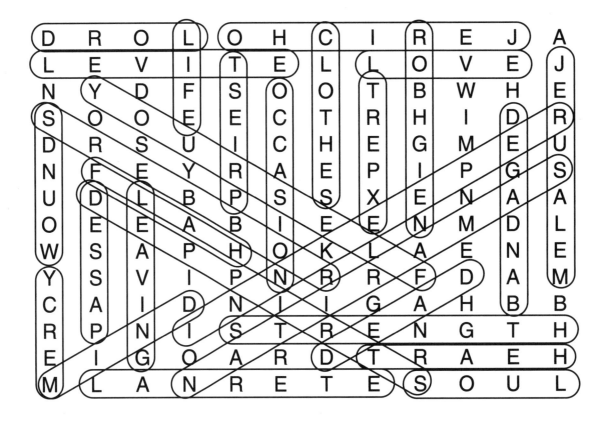

Example: Find OCCASION by counting down 3 rows and then across 6 columns.

OCCASION (3,6) EXPERT (8,8) ETERNAL (14,8) LIFE (1,4) LOVE (2,8)

LORD (1,4) HEART (13,12) SOUL (14,9) STRENGTH (12,5) MIND (14,1)

NEIGHBOR (8,9) YOURSELF (3,2) JERUSALEM (2,12) JERICHO (1,11)

ROBBERS (10,7) STRIPPED (14,9) CLOTHES (1,7) LEAVING (7,3) HALF (9,5)

DEAD (13,7) PRIEST (7,5) LEVITE (2,1) PASSED (12,2) SAMARITAN (6,12)

BANDAGED (11,11) WOUNDS (9,1) INNKEEPER (12,4) MERCY (14,1)

Jesus Visits Mary and Martha
Luke 10:38-42

Two sisters, Mary and Martha, and their brother, Lazarus, lived in Bethany, a village near Jerusalem. They were Jesus' friends. When He visited them, Martha got upset because her sister chose to listen to Jesus rather than help her prepare a meal. Jesus said that Mary's choice was better. Solve the secret phrase to find out what we should say when we are torn between spending time with God or with other things in our lives.

JESUS	MARTHA	FEET	WORK	NEEDED
DISCIPLES	OPENED	LISTENING	MYSELF	CHOSEN
CAME	HOUSE	WHAT	WORRIED	BETTER
VILLAGE	SISTER	SAID	UPSET	
WOMAN	MARY	DISTRACTED	MANY	
NAMED	LORDS	PREPARATIONS	THINGS	

```
I  D  E  F  W  O  P  E  N  E  D
J  D  E  A  H  T  R  A  M  V  E
S  E  I  N  A  M  E  D  I  I  D
T  I  S  S  T  C  P  Y  R  L  E
E  R  S  U  T  E  A  E  R  L  E
S  R  T  E  S  R  R  R  I  A  N
P  O  O  U  L  E  M  A  S  E  M
U  W  O  B  T  P  T  C  K  E  L
C  H  R  S  E  E  I  R  T  F  O
H  W  I  I  E  N  Y  O  C  L  E  R
O  S  I  I  T  W  N  E  S  D  D
S  G  N  I  H  T  S  A  T  I  S
E  G  H  C  H  Y  E  R  M  A  D
N  I  W  O  M  A  N  B  S  S  T
```

Secret Phrase

. . . __ __ __ __ __ __ __ __ __ . . __ __ __ __ __

__ __ __ __ __ __ __ . – Philippians 1:23

77

Jesus Visits Mary and Martha

Answers

Secret Phrase

. . . I desire to…be with Christ.

~ Philippians 1:23

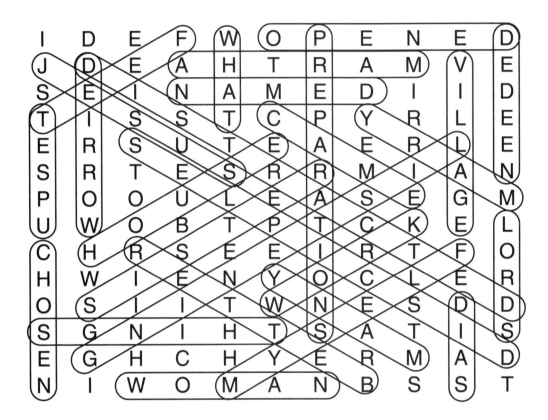

Example: Find JESUS by counting down 2 rows and then beginning in the first column.

JESUS (2,1) DISCIPLES (13,11) CAME (4,6) VILLAGE (2,10) WOMAN (14,3)

NAMED (3,4) MARTHA (2,9) OPENED (1,6) HOUSE (9,2) SISTER (11,2)

MARY (7,11) LORDS (8,11) FEET (1,4) LISTENING (5,10) WHAT (1,5)

SAID (14,10) DISTRACTED (2,2) PREPARATIONS (1,7) WORK (11,6)

MYSELF (14,5) WORRIED (8,2) UPSET (8,1) MANY (13,9) THINGS (12,6)

NEEDED (6,11) CHOSEN (9,1) BETTER (14,8)

A Son Leaves Home
Luke 15:11-24

This story is known as the parable of the prodigal son. The word "prodigal" means "wasteful." This parable could be called the story of the "wasteful" son. A person who leaves the love of God is also a wasteful person. But like the father in this story, God will always welcome back those who realize their mistakes and turn away from their sins. The secret phrase is one way of expressing how God feels when a sinner repents and turns back to Him.

YOUNGER   WILD   STOMACH   SINNED   ALIVE

SHARE   LIVING   PODS   WORTHY   LOST

DISTANT   FAMINE   HIRED   FATHER   FOUND

COUNTRY   FEED   FOOD   COMPASSION   CELEBRATE

SQUANDERED PIGS   SPARE   KISSED

WEALTH   FILL   STARVING   DEAD

```
Y  H  T  R  O  W  I  H  L  A  V  E
D  T  S  F  T  F  O  O  E  E  K  S
F  L  U  T  A  N  S  T  R  G  I  P
D  A  I  N  A  T  A  A  D  N  S  A
N  E  M  W  H  R  H  T  N  I  S  R
U  W  R  I  B  S  V  E  S  V  E  E
O  M  R  E  N  Y  D  I  R  I  D  Y
F  E  L  L  D  E  E  F  N  L  D  O
D  E  Y  R  T  N  U  O  C  G  F  U
C  V  C  O  M  P  A  S  S  I  O  N
P  I  G  S  O  O  S  U  L  T  O  G
S  L  H  D  E  A  D  L  Q  E  D  E
E  A  S  H  C  A  M  O  T  S  P  R
```

Secret Phrase

. . . "__ _____ _____ __ _____

__ __ __ __ __ ." – Luke 15:6

A Son Leaves Home

Answers

Secret Phrase

. . . "I have found my lost sheep."

~ Luke 15:6

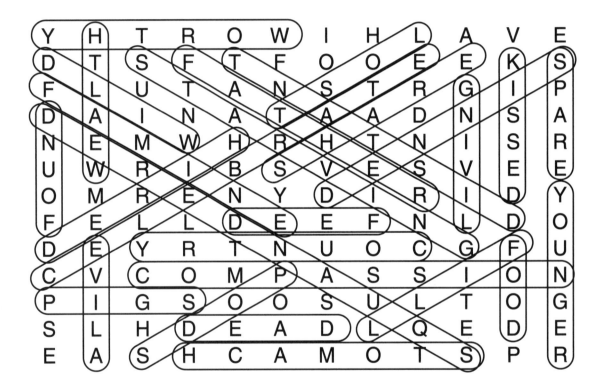

Example: Find YOUNGER by counting down 7 rows and then across 12 columns.

YOUNGER (7,12) SHARE (6,6) DISTANT (8,11) COUNTRY (9,9) SQUANDERED (13,10)
WEALTH (6,2) WILD (5,4) LIVING (8,10) FAMINE (3,1) FEED (8,8) PIGS (11,1)
FILL (9,11) STOMACH (13,10) PODS (10,6) HIRED (5,5) FOOD (9,11) SPARE (2,12)
STARVING (2,3) SINNED (2,12) WORTHY (1,6) FATHER (2,4) COMPASSION (10,3)
KISSED (2,11) DEAD (12,4) ALIVE (13,2) LOST (1,9) FOUND (8,1) CELEBRATE (10,1)

Jesus Blesses Little Children

Luke 18:15-17

Have you ever sung "Jesus Loves the Little Children"? This story shows that the song is true! Jesus' disciples thought little children might be a bother to the Lord. Instead, He encouraged children to gather around Him. The secret phrase shows how Jesus used the example of a child to teach His disciples.

PEOPLE	DISCIPLES	CHILDREN	TRUTH
BRINGING	REBUKED	COME	ANYONE
BABIES	JESUS	HINDER	WILL
HAVE	CALLED	KINGDOM	RECEIVE
TOUCH	SAID	BELONGS	NEVER
THEM	LITTLE	SUCH	ENTER

```
H   E   N   O   Y   N   A   S   E   S   C   A
C   O   M   E   L   L   G   E   M   E   H   T
J   A   E   D   R   N   A   L   L   I   C   I
E   T   L   R   O   D   H   T   T   B   U   L
S   R   K   L   E   E   L   T   R   A   S   C
U   E   E   I   E   T   H   I   U   B   I   L
S   B   L   D   N   D   N   L   H   R   A   N
D   U   H   P   W   G   A   E   E   C   T   D
H   K   S   A   I   D   D   L   I   N   M   T
S   E   T   N   L   C   P   O   E   A   H   O
N   D   G   D   L   O   S   V   M   A   A   U
M   O   N   R   E   C   E   I   V   E   G   C
T   H   E   P   M   R   R   E   D   N   I   H
```

Secret Phrase

__ _____ _ _____

_____ ___ ___ ___

_____ _____ _____.

— Matthew 18:2

81

Jesus Blesses Little Children

Answers

Secret Phrase

He called a little child and had him stand among them.

~ Matthew 18:2

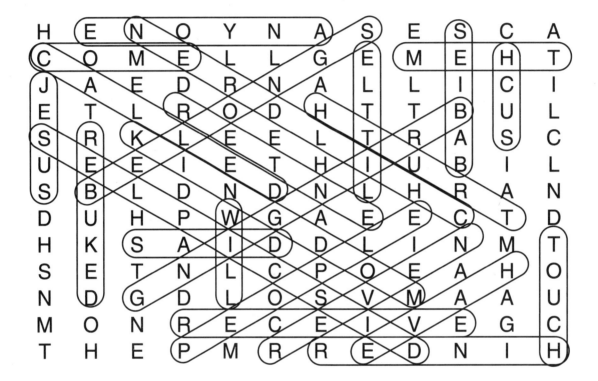

Example: Find PEOPLE by counting down 13 rows and then across 4 columns.

PEOPLE (13,4) BRINGING (4,10) BABIES (6,10) HAVE (10,11) TOUCH (9,12)

THEM (2,12) DISCIPLES (13,9) REBUKED (5,2) JESUS (3,1) CALLED (2,1)

SAID (9,3) LITTLE (7,8) CHILDREN (8,10) COME (2,1) HINDER (13,12)

KINGDOM (5,3) BELONGS (7,2) SUCH (5,11) TRUTH (8,11) ANYONE (1,7)

WILL (8,5) RECEIVE (12,4) NEVER (9,10) ENTER (8,8)

A Blind Man Receives Sight
Luke 18:35-43

When asked if He was the Savior, Jesus answered, "The blind receive sight, the lame walk, those who have leprosy are cured, the deaf hear, the dead are raised, and the good news is preached to the poor" (Matthew 11:5). Only one sent from God could do such miracles! Here is the story of one of those miracles. The secret phrase repeats what Jesus said could happen to those who follow Him.

APPROACHED	CROWD	PASSING	SHOUTED	SIGHT
JERICHO	GOING	CALLED	ORDERED	FOLLOWED
BLIND	ASKED	MERCY	BROUGHT	PEOPLE
ROADSIDE	HAPPENING	REBUKED	CAME	ALSO
BEGGING	JESUS	QUIET	NEAR	PRAISED
HEARD	NAZARETH	STOPPED	RECEIVED	

```
T  H  T  H  G  I  S  E  C  A  M  E
B  S  U  S  E  J  E  L  P  O  E  P
L  D  E  L  L  A  C  D  W  O  R  C
D  E  H  C  A  O  R  P  P  A  C  I
E  N  D  A  L  S  O  D  I  N  Y  D
P  R  I  I  P  A  S  S  I  N  G  D
P  F  E  L  S  P  E  D  A  O  E  C
O  O  J  Q  B  D  E  Z  I  T  G  T
T  L  E  U  E  V  A  N  U  I  N  H
S  L  R  I  I  R  G  O  I  V  I  G
N  O  I  E  E  E  H  S  R  N  G  U
E  W  C  T  A  S  K  E  D  I  G  O
A  E  H  G  H  D  E  K  U  B  E  R
R  D  O  R  D  E  R  E  D  T  B  B
```

Secret Phrase

. . . "___ ___ ___ ___ ___ ___ ___ ___ ___ ___ ___

___ ___ ___ ___ ___ ___." . .   – Luke 7:22

A Blind Man Receives Sight

Answers

Secret Phrase

. . . "The blind receive sight." . . .

~ Luke 7:22

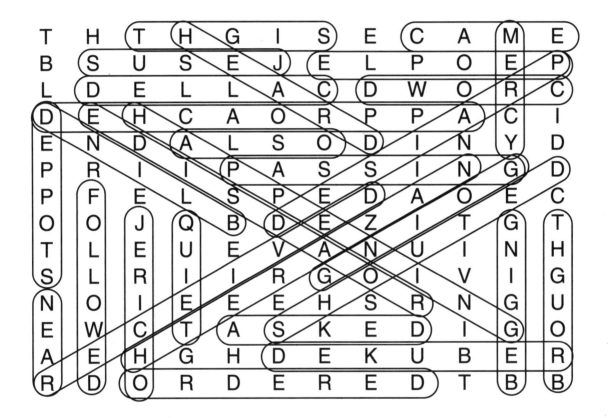

Example: Find APPROACHED by counting down 4 rows and then across 10 columns.

APPROACHED (4,10) JERICHO (8,3) BLIND (8,5) ROADSIDE (11,9)

BEGGING (14,11) HEARD (1,4) CROWD (3,12) GOING (6,11) ASKED (12,5)

HAPPENING (4,3) JESUS (2,6) NAZARETH (6,10) PASSING (6,5) CALLED (3,7)

MERCY (1,11) REBUKED (13,12) QUIET (8,4) STOPPED (10,1) SHOUTED (12,6)

ORDERED (14,3) BROUGHT (14,12) CAME (1,9) NEAR (11,1) RECEIVED (14,1)

SIGHT (1,7) FOLLOWED (7,2) PEOPLE (2,12) ALSO (5,4) PRAISED (2,12)

Zaccaeus Climbs a Tree
Luke 19:1-10

Zaccaeus had become wealthy as the main tax collector in Jericho. Tax collectors were another group of people that the Jews avoided. Yet Jesus not only talked with Zaccaeus but went to his home. Zaccaeus was a short person. The secret phrase tells why Zaccaeus climbed a tree.

▬ ▬

JERICHO	CROWD	IMMEDIATELY	BACK	SEEK
ZACCHAEUS	CLIMBED	STAY	FOUR	SAVE
CHIEF	SYCAMORE	WELCOMED	TIMES	LOST
COLLECTOR	TREE	GLADLY	SALVATION	
WEALTHY	JESUS	LORD	HOUSE	
SHORT	LOOKED	ANYTHING	ABRAHAM	

▬ ▬

```
H E W A N T C E D T G J
F O H C I R E J D L O E
D E K O O L S E A E I S
G T I W Z L M D K M Y U
N R D H A O L S M C S S
I O E W C Y M E A H A O
H H I L C A D M C Y V B
T S E T H I O I A T E L
Y W T A A R J T S E O O
N S R T E V S O F O U R
A B E S U C L I M B E D
A L E E S W E A L T H O Y
Y U S W K A S E S U O H
```

Secret Phrase

__ __ __ __ __ __ __ __ __ __ __ __ __ __ __ __

__ __ __ __ __ __ __ __ __ __ __ . . . .   - Luke 19:3

Zacchaeus Climbs a Tree

Answers

Secret Phrase

He wanted to see who Jesus was. . . .

~ Luke 19:3

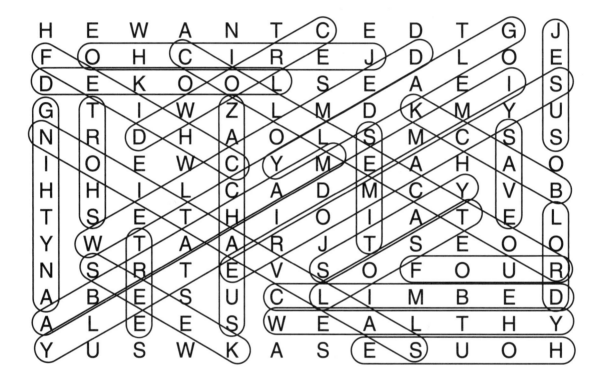

Example: Find JERICHO by counting down 2 rows and then across 8 columns.

JERICHO (2,8) ZACCHAEUS (4,5) CHIEF (6,5) COLLECTOR (2,4) WEALTHY (12,6)

SHORT (8,2) CROWD (1,7) CLIMBED (11,6) SYCAMORE (3,12) TREE (9,3)

JESUS (1,12) LOOKED (3,6) IMMEDIATELY (3,11) STAY (10,7) WELCOMED (9,2)

GLADLY (1,11) LORD (8,12) ANYTHING (11,1) BACK (7,12) FOUR (10,9)

TIMES (9,8) SALVATION (13,9) HOUSE (13,12) ABRAHAM (12,1) SEEK (10,2)

SAVE (5,11) LOST (11,7)

A Hero's Welcome
Mark 11:1-11

Jesus visited Jerusalem several times, but this occasion was an especially festive event. People lined the streets and shouted praises in His name. As a sign of honor, they placed palm branches and their cloaks along the roadway. But the rulers were jealous of Jesus receiving so much honor and praise. They decided that they must destroy Him. Solve the secret phrase to find out what the people shouted joyfully at Jesus as He passed by.

BETHANY	BRING	THEIR	SHOUTED	DAVID
MOUNT	SEND	CLOAKS	HOSANNA	JESUS
OLIVES	BACK	SPREAD	BLESSED	ENTERED
DISCIPLES	SHORTLY	ROAD	COMING	TEMPLE
VILLAGE	UNTIED	BRANCHES	KINGDOM	
COLT	THREW	AHEAD	FATHER	

```
B  L  A  R  S  E  V  I  L  O  Y  E
B  E  N  T  E  R  E  D  S  L  S  S
E  R  N  D  L  H  I  L  T  S  P  M
T  S  A  G  P  H  T  R  P  R  E  O
K  H  S  N  I  I  O  A  E  M  D  U
N  O  O  I  C  H  G  A  F  N  E  N
W  U  H  R  S  H  D  B  E  W  C  T
H  T  O  B  I  D  E  S  S  E  L  B
C  E  T  O  D  T  I  S  D  R  O  M
E  D  G  H  H  J  T  G  A  H  A  S
I  N  T  A  E  T  N  H  E  T  K  E
N  A  N  S  L  I  U  M  H  E  S  O
F  Y  U  O  M  L  R  O  A  D  T  H
E  S  C  O  L  K  I  N  G  D  O  M
B  A  C  K  O  D  I  V  A  D  R  D
```

Secret Phrase

" __ __ __ __ __ __ __ __ __ __ __ __ __ __ __ __ __

__ __ __ __ __ __ __ __ __ __ __ __ __ __ __ __

__ __ __ __ __ __ __ __ __ __ __ ___!" . . .   – Luke 19:38

A Hero's Welcome

Answers

Secret Phrase

"Blessed is the king who comes in the name of the Lord!" . . .

~ Luke 19:38

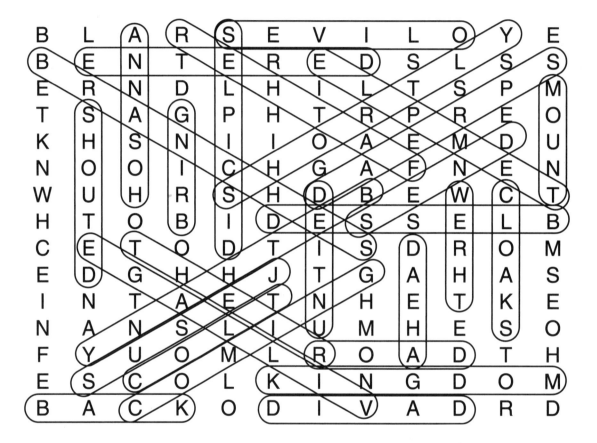

Example: Find BETHANY by counting down 7 rows and then across 8 columns.

BETHANY (7,8) MOUNT (3,12) OLIVES (1,10) DISCIPLES (9,5) VILLAGE (15,8)

COLT (14,3) BRING (8,4) SEND (8,8) BACK (15,1) SHORTLY (7,5) UNTIED (12,7)

THREW (11,10) THEIR (9,3) CLOAKS (7,11) SPREAD (2,12) ROAD (13,7)

BRANCHES (2,1) AHEAD (13,9) SHOUTED (4,2) HOSANNA (7,3) BLESSED (8,12)

COMING (15,3) KINGDOM (14,6) FATHER (6,9) DAVID (15,10) JESUS (10,6)

ENTERED (2,2) TEMPLE (7,12)

Eating in an Upper Room
Mark 14:12-26

The Jews observed a special meal called Passover. It was a special day to remember when Moses led the Israelites out of slavery in Egypt. Jesus and His apostles ate the meal in an upper room. Only a few hours later, the authorities arrested Him. That meal in the upper room became known as the "Last Supper." Discover if Jesus knew what was about to happen by filling in the secret phrase.

LARGE	EVENING	THANKS	BLOOD	HYMN
UPPER	TWELVE	BROKE	COVENANT	MOUNT
ROOM	BETRAY	BODY	FRUIT	OLIVES
FURNISHED	SADDENED	GAVE	VINE	
READY	JESUS	OFFERED	KINGDOM	
PREPARED	BREAD	DRANK	SUNG	

```
J  D  R  E  T  H  A  N  K  S  S  B
U  R  E  S  S  G  K  I  N  E  R  H
T  A  P  H  E  A  N  W  N  E  Y  T
H  N  P  Y  S  G  D  I  A  M  A  B
Y  K  U  D  D  I  V  D  N  D  C  R
D  D  O  O  L  B  N  E  E  E  O  O
A  T  M  B  M  O  O  R  S  N  V  K
E  G  R  A  L  H  A  E  U  U  E  E
R  I  S  I  H  P  O  F  S  F  N  D
U  E  V  L  E  W  T  F  E  V  A  G
B  E  T  R  A  Y  R  O  J  W  N  A
S  S  P  C  O  M  F  R  U  I  T  E
```

Secret Phrase

__ __ __ __ __ __   __ __ __ __   __ __ __ __   __ __ __

__ __ __ __ __   __ __ __   __ __ __ __ .   – from John 13:1

Eating in an Upper Room

Answers

Secret Phrase

Jesus knew that his hour was come.

~ from John 13:1

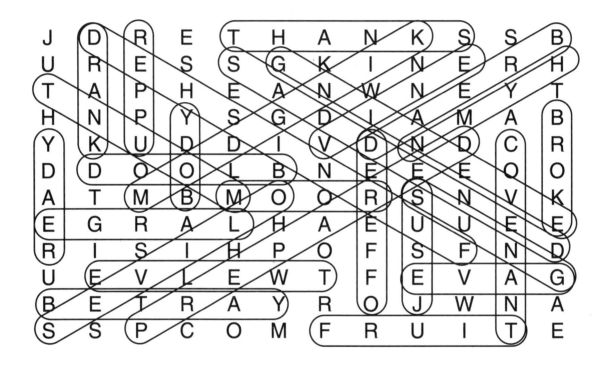

Example: Find LARGE by counting down 8 rows and then across 5 columns.

LARGE (8,5) UPPER (5,3) ROOM (7,8) FURNISHED (9,10) READY (9,1)

PREPARED (12,3) EVENING (8,12) TWELVE (10,7) BETRAY (11,1)

SADDENED (2,5) JESUS (11,9) BREAD (1,12) THANKS (1,5) BROKE (4,12)

BODY (7,4) GAVE (10,12) OFFERED (11,8) DRANK (1,2) BLOOD (6,6)

COVENANT (5,11) FRUIT (12,7) VINE (5,7) KINGDOM (1,9) SUNG (7,9)

HYMN (2,12) MOUNT (7,5) OLIVES (7,6)

Peter Denies Jesus
Luke 22:54-62

At the Last Supper, Peter said, "Lord, I am ready to go with You to prison and to death." However, before the night was over, Peter claimed that he did not even know Jesus. As he made the last denial, the rooster crowed as Jesus said it would. Write the unused letters in the blanks of the secret phrase to learn what Peter did when the rooster crowed.

PETER	SERVANT	LATER	GALILEAN	TURNED
FOLLOWED	GIRL	SOMEONE	REPLIED	DISOWN
DISTANCE	LOOKED	ANOTHER	SPEAKING	THREE
KINDLED	CLOSELY	ASSERTED	ROOSTER	TIMES
FIRE	DENIED	CERTAINLY	CROWED	WEPT
TOGETHER	WOMAN	FELLOW	LORD	BITTERLY

```
D  B  I  T  T  E  R  L  Y  P  T  P  E  W
L  I  E  E  T  D  E  L  D  N  I  K  N  T
O  G  S  E  R  T  N  A  V  R  E  S  O  H
O  N  R  T  W  I  R  E  N  R  R  G  E  R
K  I  M  O  A  R  F  A  E  E  E  M  M  E
E  K  M  T  E  N  E  S  B  T  P  E  O  E
D  A  R  T  R  L  C  S  H  S  L  E  S  D
N  E  E  L  I  A  R  E  C  O  I  R  N  D
C  P  W  L  O  E  R  R  H  O  E  E  I  B
R  S  A  O  H  R  O  T  O  R  D  K  L  G
E  G  D  T  L  W  D  E  N  I  E  D  A  O
C  L  O  S  E  L  Y  D  E  N  R  U  T  W
N  N  A  D  I  S  O  W  N  T  I  M  E  S
A  N  W  O  L  L  E  F  D  W  E  P  R  T
```

Secret Phrase

.. __ __ __ __ __   __ __ __ __ __ __ __ __ __ __ .. __ __ __

__ __ __ __ __ __ __ __ __ __ __ __ __ __ __ __ __ __ __ .

Peter Denies Jesus

Answers

Secret Phrase

. . . Peter remembered...and he broke down and wept.

~ Mark 14:72

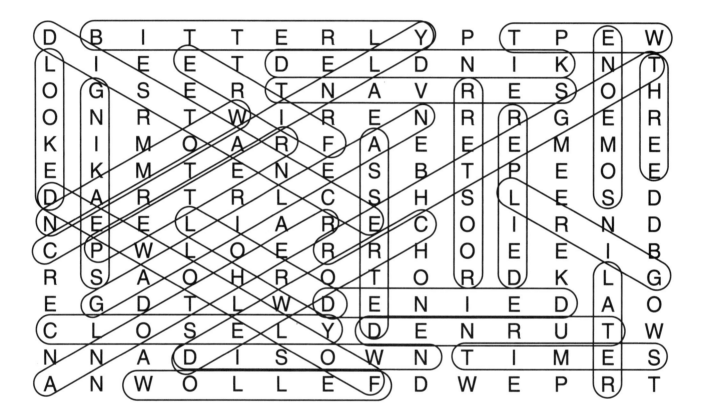

Example: Find PETER by counting down 9 rows and then across 2 column.

PETER (9,2) FOLLOWED (14,8) DISTANCE (1,1) KINDLED (2,12) FIRE (5,7)

TOGETHER (2,14) SERVANT (3,12) GIRL (10,14) LOOKED (2,1) CLOSELY (12,1)

DENIED (11,7) WOMAN (4,5) LATER (10,13) SOMEONE (7,13) ANOTHER (14,1)

ASSERTED (5,8) CERTAINLY (9,1) FELLOW (14,8) GALILEAN (11,2) REPLIED (4,11)

SPEAKING (10,2) ROOSTER (10,10) CROWED (8,9) LORD (8,4) TURNED (12,13)

DISOWN (13,4) THREE (2,14) TIMES (13,10) WEPT (1,14) BITTERLY (1,2)

The Terrible Deed
Luke 23:26-49

E vil people put the Son of God to death. They nailed Him to a cross. They had resented His popularity, His message of love and His teaching that He had come to save the world. They thought they could get rid of Him by killing Him. They were wrong! Solve the secret phrase to read the mocking sign that Pilate had fastened to the cross.

▬▬ ▬▬

SIMON	CRUCIFIED	DIVIDED	SAVED	JEWS
CROSS	RIGHT	CLOTHES	OTHERS	LAND
PEOPLE	LEFT	CASTING	SOLDIERS	EARTH
WOMEN	FATHER	LOTS	MOCKED	COMMIT
MOURNED	FORGIVE	RULERS	WRITTEN	SPIRIT
SKULL	THEM	SNEERED	KING	

▬▬ ▬▬

```
S  S  O  R  C  W  J  E  D  T  H  S
E  O  U  S  O  O  R  E  H  T  A  F
H  M  L  M  M  F  I  G  R  S  N  D
T  A  E  D  M  F  I  A  P  M  N  Z
O  N  S  H  I  R  E  I  O  A  S  A
L  F  K  C  T  E  R  U  L  E  R  S
C  O  U  R  G  I  R  N  D  E  E  W
T  R  L  D  T  N  E  S  E  H  H  E
C  G  L  D  T  E  I  L  K  S  T  J
H  I  E  D  T  D  P  K  C  I  O  K
L  V  I  I  N  O  I  G  O  M  O  F
D  E  R  E  E  N  S  V  M  O  T  H
E  W  F  P  C  A  S  T  I  N  G  J
E  L  O  T  S  S  A  V  E  D  W  S
```

Secret Phrase

... _____ _____ _____, _____

_____ _____ _____ _____.   **-John 19:19**

93

The Terrible Deed

Answers

Secret Phrase

. . . Jesus of Nazareth, the king of the Jews.

~ John 19:19

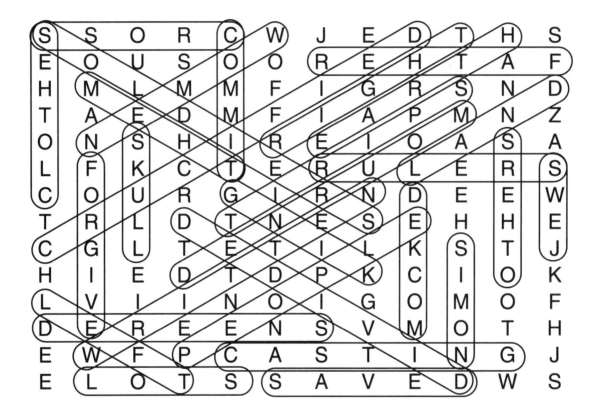

Example: Find SIMON by counting down 9 rows and then across 10 columns.

SIMON (9,10) CROSS (1,5) PEOPLE (13,4) WOMEN (1,6) MOURNED (4,10)

SKULL (5,3) CRUCIFIED (9,1) RIGHT (5,6) LEFT (11,1) FATHER (2,12)

FORGIVE (6,2) THEM (6,5) DIVIDED (14,10) CLOTHES (7,1) CASTING (13,5)

LOTS (14,2) RULERS (6,7) SNEERED (12,7) SAVED (14,6) OTHERS (10,11)

SOLDIERS (1,1) MOCKED (12,9) WRITTEN (13,2) KING (10,8) JEWS (9,12)

LAND (6,9) EARTH (5,7) COMMIT (1,5) SPIRIT (3,10)

Jesus Lives!
Mark 16:1-15

Jesus' death was not the end of the story! Early on Sunday morning, some women went to the tomb and found that it was empty. Jesus had risen from the dead! Solve the secret phrase to discover what an angel told the women. After Jesus arose, His disciples traveled the world to tell about the Good News.

MAGDALENE	FIRST	WHITE	TREMBLING	CREATION
MARY	SUNRISE	ROBE	FLED	
MOTHER	STONE	JESUS	APPEARED	
JAMES	ROLLED	NAZARENE	WORLD	
SALOME	SITTING	CRUCIFIED	PREACH	
EARLY	DRESSED	RISEN	NEWS	

```
H  E  E  S  I  R  N  U  S  I  S  N
O  D  N  G  R  O  B  E  G  W  N  T
H  R  E  N  E  R  D  E  N  O  E  H
E  E  L  I  A  H  A  E  I  O  S  N
R  S  A  T  F  Z  S  T  L  I  T  A
S  S  D  T  E  I  A  N  B  F  P  S
J  E  G  I  R  E  C  R  M  P  E  U
F  D  A  S  R  S  T  U  E  A  P  A
I  S  M  C  H  E  S  A  R  N  R  D
R  M  O  T  H  E  R  L  T  C  E  L
S  A  L  O  M  E  Y  R  A  M  A  R
T  S  A  A  D  E  L  L  O  R  C  O
I  D  J  E  S  U  S  E  T  I  H  W
```

Secret Phrase

__ __   __ __   __ __ __   __ __ __ __;   __ __   __ __ __ __   __ __   __ __   __ __ __ ____...

– Matthew 28:6

Jesus Lives!

Answers

Secret Phrase

He is not here; he has risen, just as he said. . . .

~ Matthew 28:6

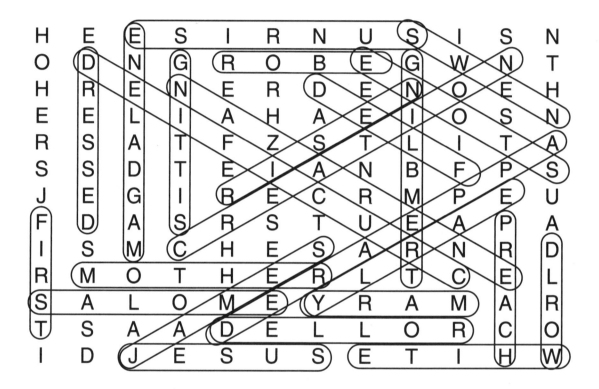

Example: Find MAGDALENE by counting down 9 rows and then across 3 columns.

MAGDALENE (9,3) MARY (11,10) MOTHER (10,2) JAMES (13,3) SALOME (11,1)

EARLY (7,11) FIRST (8,1) SUNRISE (1,9) STONE (6,12) ROLLED (12,10) SITTING (8,4)

DRESSED (2,2) WHITE (13,12) ROBE (2,5) JESUS (13,3) NAZARENE (3,4)

CRUCIFIED (10,10) RISEN (7,5) TREMBLING (10,9) FLED (6,10) APPEARED (5,12)

WORLD (13,12) PREACH (8,11) NEWS (4,12) CREATION (9,4)